THE HEART

OF THE

RUNAWAY

BY LIBERTY ELIAS MILLER

This book is for everyone - all of you who have loved me, and all of you who have hurt me. Without each of those experiences I would not be who, or where, I am today. Thank you for all the laughter, and all the tears.

For my mother, Cherry - for teaching me how to fight and survive. The strength you instilled within me has been my greatest resource in life.

For my dad, Bruce - for teaching me how to smile and be kind. Without your light, my world would have stayed engulfed in darkness.

And for my brother, Bern. Your story deserved to be told.

Foreword

Nothing about Liberty Miller's life showed in her face when we met. Dressed like a punk rock kid, and with the blazing enthusiasm of a pirate captain, there was no way of knowing her blood-spattered, dizzy, heartbreaking history. She wasn't evasive, shy or secretive in the least, far from it. She didn't seem wounded, and certainly didn't shrink from anything. Bright-eyed and bold, she seemed like someone who would easily and fluidly skip right past small talk and dive into the deep water where the good stuff lurks. There was no way for me to know how much pain had gone into the careful construction of that person. I knew she seemed inexplicably trustworthy, and that we shared a mutual adoration for the power of music. For me, at the time, that was enough to know.

We met during a long and grueling road trip with my band at a time when I often didn't know which city I was in. In emails, she asked if there was anything she could do to help the band out. I explained that touring in an unsigned band, living out of a van, means we can use all the help we can get. Before I knew it, she was hanging posters around town, calling radio stations about the show, even selling shirts for us at the club. She became a one-woman army, a Swiss army knife of indie-band help. While we set up for the show, she would meticulously construct a display of our merchandise, somehow find lamps to light the shirts in dark clubs, then worked all night to sell all she could. This kind of fire is rarely seen, even among professionals, let alone those who "just want to help."

One of the first conversations we ever had began with her asking, "I'm at a fork in the road where I can throw out everything – my marriage, my job, all I know and love that makes me feel safe, all to go try to stop the slaughter of dolphins. Or I can stick with what I know and make it work. How can I know what the right choice is?" That was how she let me know that we were never going to talk about the weather.

Over the years we discussed life choices, the difficulty in keeping hope for humanity smoldering in your chest, and the importance of music to our sanity. She never shied away from anything. When she worked for my band at our shows I would see throughout the night, by the glow of the merch booth lights, the drunks and celebrants, half-deaf and yelling at her even when the music had long since ended. She took it all in stride with a glowing smile. Once, when I pointed out how impressed I was with her ability to keep a cool head in the chaotic whirlpool of the rock scene, she laughed and said, "It's for a good cause. I love to help." That was when I realized that Libby walked through this world differently than most. Not looking for what she could get, but what she could give. Not seeking what she needed, but what needed her. "I don't know what you're going to do with your life," I told her, "but I know it's going to be amazing."

Robert Wynia is the frontman for the Portland, Oregon band, Floater.

Chapter One

"Looking back across the years, at a million unshed tears. How could I have held them all?" Floater

As I sank below the surface, I watched the rays of Mediterranean sunlight illuminate the jellyfish that had just paralyzed me with their venom. There seemed to be hundreds of them, squishing their way through the blue water. Tiny little jellies with milky white bells and brilliant purple dots. They looked so tranquil.

My mind was screaming at my body to swim, to reach the surface and breathe, but it was useless. I watched the jellies through the fogged-up glass of my snorkel mask and simply let myself go. I don't remember my lungs burning for air or being afraid of drowning. All I remember is a serene sense of peace.

A blur of arms and hands disturbed the water before me. I felt something grab me and pull me towards the surface as I stared into the blackness of the sea beneath me – the blackness where I had been sinking only moments before. My crewmates hauled me onto the deck of the ship where the doctor waited with a knife to scrape the nettles from my arm and a bottle of vinegar to douse me with. I had never felt such searing pain in all my life. I sat stoically while the feeling of fire raged inside my flesh, and my mind filled with horror stories of respiratory problems from jellyfish stings.

Later that night, I admitted how much it hurt while James held me in his arms, soothing me with his Australian accent. I was so used to my husband leaving the room when I cried that to finally be held by a man who kissed away my tears made me cry even harder. Never mind that my husband and I were currently in different countries, on different continents, separated by a million miles of misunderstanding, a lack of communication, and burnt-out love. I was in a small cabin on a ship in the middle of the ocean, being held by another man – a man I had so deeply and accidentally fallen in love with. But we'll come back to that.

***

The aloneness I've felt inside has haunted me since my first days on this earth. It feels as if I were born into a world where I'm not welcome, and the exhaustion of pretending that this life doesn't hurt me is overwhelming sometimes. The unwelcomed feeling, combined with a near-crippling fear of abandonment, has created within me a need to be needed; a need to feel important, wanted; a need that has caused me to seek out love and acceptance in all the wrong places. I feel as if I have never truly been understood by the people around me, and as soon as I was able, I started moving from state to state, from country to country, all the while holding on to the hope that someday I would find a place where I fit in.

For a brief moment in time, I found that place with the Sea Shepherd Conservation Society (SSCS), and while I had it, it was the single most beautiful thing I had ever experienced. And while I was struggling with my inner questionings of Sea Shepherd and their values as a non-profit, I still was reveling in the glory of where I was, all the while banishing my doubts about the organization and the people who controlled it to the deepest corners of my mind. Eventually, light was shed upon those dark corners, and my doubts about Sea Shepherd became impossible to ignore.

For me, it all began in 2009, with a documentary about a dolphin slaughter in Japan (documentary, The Cove) and a TV show about stopping whale hunting in Antarctica (Animal Planet's, Whale Wars). My husband and I would watch Whale Wars and I would proclaim "that's what I want to do!", never imagining that one day I actually would do it.

Never did I desire to obtain the "American Dream" of working 9-5 at a corporation, owning a home, making car payments and taking yearly vacations in Hawaii while signing online petitions to stop the destruction of our world, the overfishing of our seas, the large and small environmental injustices that occur on a daily basis. I wanted to get my hands dirty, to be in the field, actively fighting for my beliefs in animal rights and marine conservation, no matter how great the danger.

However, I found myself, at the age of 29, living the exact life I had never wanted, and I harbored a horrid suffocating feeling - a knowing that I wasn't meant to live a mundane life; that I was meant for greatness. In the middle of my quarter life crisis I was overcome with a sense that it was now or never. Death has surrounded me since I was very young, and I've learned the valuable lesson that any moment can be your last, and that the need to live the life you desire to its fullest is very real.

My husband was a good man, but he wasn't the right man. And though I've never regretted my decision to leave, following my dreams took its toll, and I paid with mostly tears and blood. After years of feeling incredibly trapped, it took only one week for me to decide to radically change my life and board a plane to Japan, where I spent four months at the Cove as a foreign correspondent and campaign leader for Sea Shepherd, protesting one of the most horrific dolphin slaughters on the planet. It was an opportunity that had dropped unexpectedly out of the sky and landed in my hands. It was my opportunity to finally make those childhood dreams of doing something great with my life become a reality.

My husband didn't stop me from walking out the front door of our house. He just let me go. He sat on the couch, and simply watched me leave. It was a crushing feeling, standing in the open doorway of the home we had purchased in lieu of a honeymoon, our Nissan Xterra sitting in the driveway loaded with my personal possessions, and peering at him while he sat on the couch, silently willing him to ask me to stay. I gazed at my little family gathered there in the living room: our dog, our two cats, my husband, all of them watching me walk away from the life we had built. The dog whined while the cats circled my feet, confused about what was happening and begging me to stay with their sad eyes. But there sat my husband, bouncing his knee up and down like he always used to do and playing video games, unable to even press pause as his wife walked out the door for the final time.

He knew that all I wanted was for him to ask me to stay. How many times had I told him that I would stay if he were only willing to talk to me? I didn't ask him to fix our problems. I didn't ask him to make things perfect. I didn't even ask him to talk about our problems. All I asked was for him to have a conversation with me. A normal, everyday "how was work?" kind of conversation. But he didn't, he couldn't, or he wouldn't, and I came to the realization that it was wrong of me to want him to change. He wasn't a talker, and that's okay; I see that now, but all I saw back then was my loneliness. So I walked out, and one mile down the road I pulled over and sobbed; the deep, sorrowful shuttering that made me feel as though the world around me was ending. I've never been one to cry without reserve, but there, on the side of that road, alone in the vehicle that had taken us so many places together, I finally let go and cried all the bitter and burning tears that I had been collecting inside myself during the years of my lonely marriage.

The feeling of so desperately wanting my husband to understand, of wanting him to reach out and then finally realizing that he wasn't going to, was crushing. I felt as if I were constantly struggling to save someone's life, his and mine, ours, but I was always being pulled beneath the surface. In the end, I realized I was fighting to breathe, to simply stay afloat, and that everything else was already lost. We had drifted away from each other a long time ago and now I needed to focus on my own survival. I felt like a child inside, not knowing which direction to turn, not knowing what action to take to make him understand how I was feeling.

My words failed me desperately during our weekly marriage counseling sessions that lasted nearly a year. Frustration, fear and deep love forced tears from my eyes, coming in waves of heaving sobs accompanied by pleas for him to reach out, to open up. Time and again our therapist would bluntly state to my husband that his wife was going to leave him if he didn't talk, but still he simply sat there, bouncing his knee, unable to take action. One of the only times he opened up during our counseling sessions was to irritably say that he didn't understand why he couldn't simply buy me a new car and have me be happy. His love language was gift-giving, and it made me feel as if he were trying to buy my silence about my unhappiness. It's now an unpleasant trigger for me when a man gives me too many gifts.

But if I focus on being honest, I don't believe I truly wanted things to change. All I could concentrate on at that point in time was freedom; my freedom and my own survival. I wanted things to fall apart, because I wanted out.

I took the offer from Sea Shepherd and went to Japan in November of 2010. My husband and I put our decision to divorce on hold, deciding instead to see how we felt after four months apart. I quit my product photography job at Grizzly Industrial in Bellingham, Washington and crossed the Pacific Ocean alone, 30,000 feet above the earth. In the process of destroying the life I had created, I felt like my true life was finally beginning, and it was all so much more beautiful and heartbreaking than I could ever have imagined.

***

I will never be able to find the words to describe what I witnessed at the Cove in Taiji, Japan, a place where dolphins are rounded up daily, from September through March, and massacred (watch the Academy Award winning documentary, The Cove). I will always carry with me the raw and brutal emotions I experienced there; the gut-wrenching barbaric slaughter that I watched with my own eyes, and the horrid, excruciating sounds of sheer terror emitted from the dolphins as their lives were torn away from them, accompanied by the deafening silence of death.

My four months at the Cove in Japan make up a time in my life that will always stay with me, good and bad. I crossed paths with amazing people that I never would have otherwise. I'm proud of the work I did there, even if I'm no longer proud of the organization I worked with, and I'm proud of the majority of the people who stood at the Cove with me.

However, it was also a time in my life that caused much damage. I walked away from everything that was known, familiar and comfortable to me. My husband and I talked once during the months I was at the Cove. When he picked me up at the Seattle airport in March of 2011, it was clear that our marriage was over.

The next morning, we sat at the kitchen table and decided to go our separate ways. I had been offered the opportunity to join Sea Shepherd aboard their flagship, the M/Y Steve Irwin, as a photographer and deckhand and needed health insurance to do so. Though we were separating, we decided to stay legally married, so I could remain on his health care policy. It would be nearly a year before we divorced.

The severity of the emotional trauma that naturally accompanies standing at the Cove was an overwhelming shock that I had not been prepared for, but never had I felt so fulfilled and complete; my activism and conservation work were the fuel that drove my life and I've never regretted the decisions I made in regard to pursing my passion, my dream, and my beliefs.

Upon my return to the United States, during the brief months I was home before joining the Steve Irwin, I became overwhelmed with such intense depression and PTSD that I couldn't form a complete thought in my head, let alone complete sentences. The smallest thing would catapult me straight back to Taiji in my mind's eye and I would drift into a daze of oblivion, even in the middle of a conversation. I struggled, and fortunately, thanks in part to the support and encouragement of my parents, I had the sense to seek medical help when my mom suggested it, but I truly believe that the only thing that set my mind right again was joining the Steve Irwin and surrounding myself with the ocean and with people who understood my passion. Were it not for that nurturing environment, I don't know what would have become of my delicate mind. Professional volunteering and activism, while a rewarding way of life, is difficult beyond belief.

Chapter Two

"I'll make you feel you're made of blood in a world that's plastic"
Floater

It's shocking how the glimmer of what we perceive to be love in a man's eyes can change everything and make you feel so whole; like you were never really damaged to begin with.

I joined the Steve Irwin a damaged woman indeed. Still legally married, yet separated for many months, I was intent on embracing my newly discovered freedom, my unearthed lust for life, and digging deeper within myself as an individual and discovering what I truly wanted. I had no intention of meeting a man and had just said to my cabinmate a few nights before how proud I was of myself for not being interested in a single one of my male crewmates.

Then James walked up the gangplank in Toulon, France on June 1st, 2011 and my world was tipped upside down like a red plastic Solo cup on an empty keg at a house party, dripping out what was left of my liquefied soul.

There's moments in life that are frozen in my memory; moments that either hurt so terribly, or that created so much happiness that my mind took a snapshot of them, and I see them as clearly as if I were looking at a photograph. The emotions of those moments are there as well, coursing through my heart and soul as if they were fresh and undiluted by time.

I was walking the port side breezeway of the Steve Irwin in the shimmering heat of the Mediterranean sun when I heard his footsteps on the gangway. He had been away on holiday when I joined the ship weeks earlier and was just now returning. Of course, I had seen him on Whale Wars; I knew who he was. What I didn't know was how seeing him in the flesh would send fire and ice coursing through my veins simultaneously; how my heart would jump clear up into my throat, but also drop down to the pit of my stomach and make me gasp for air.

What followed was an unexpected whirlwind love affair that only exists in movies and books...and aboard ships floating upon the waves of the sea.

***

The first time we touched was on the skiff deck during working hours. As several of us took a break, James and I leaned against the Delta, the small inflatable boat we used to chase whale hunters and tuna poachers. He was still wearing his blue camo hardhat, and our arms touched. His right arm, my left arm. It's a girlish thing to remember; something I'm sure had no meaning to him at all. It was a light brush at first, but it became full on contact that neither of us moved away from. A crewmate took our photo at that moment.

A few days later, docked in Syracuse, Sicily, I asked James if he wanted to go for a walk with me that afternoon. I remember feeling no nervousness, no insecurity, and no shame. There were no games, no childish flirting. I asked him out, and he said yes.

We roamed that ancient city in the sparkling sunlight, surrounded by a rich and brutal history. We walked the uneven cobblestones worn by the feet of a thousand

Romans. We sat by the waterside, my bare legs dangling in the harbor while James swam in the salty sea with the local kids. We ate granitas and hid when we saw our crewmates, wanting only to share the day with each other. We laughed and made indecent jokes at my expense because I had been kicked out of a church for wearing a tank top, exposing my shoulders like a harlot. We walked, and we talked, and we laughed, and I fell in love.

When the time came for me to report back to the ship for duty that evening, James walked me to the dock, kissed me on the cheek and gave me the most heartwarming and soul-healing hug I had ever experienced. I walked back to the ship and he turned to head back to town to continue exploring. His habit of kissing my cheek would become one of my favorite things about him, and something I've wished every boyfriend since would do, but it's simply and disappointingly not an American custom.

He invited me to his cabin that night, and I went. When he leaned in to kiss me, it was surreal. In his arms was the most beautiful place to be. When he invited me to stay, I told him I wasn't ready. I went back to my own bunk that night, knowing that first I would need to tell him the truth about still being married.

***

James had the ability to make me feel like more of an adult than I've ever perceived myself to be. He made me want to be mature, responsible and well-adjusted, and while I am all those things (to an extent, at least), most often I feel like a broken little girl who's pretending to be a strong woman. He made me see that I truly am strong.

Technically being my boss, he would assign tasks to me that I didn't believe I could do; tasks that included rebuilding a dive compressor and changing out the hydraulic hoses on the crane. I questioned my ability to do them, but he never did. And so, I did them. And I did them well.

The days we were together aboard the Steve were filled with such bliss for me; such magic and romance like I had never known, and I had no desire to sabotage that with the sticky mess that feelings and emotions tend to create, so I kept my mouth shut about the vast amounts of love that were roiling inside me. I adored him, respected him, and loved him madly, and I never told him.

At least not while we were on the ship.

***

Our days were filled with wandering foreign ports, places I had only ever seen in magazines, sailing the high seas under sparkling stars, and being lulled to sleep each night by the waves and the feel of one another's body. After the workday, he would bring a blanket to the bow of the ship where we would lie in the fading Mediterranean sunshine as he read aloud to me from whatever book he was engrossed in at the time. Eventually, the stars would twinkle to life and the lights of Morocco, or Italy, or whichever landmass we were near, danced toward us across the sea. Oftentimes, he would play the fiddle, and I would close my eyes to the sweet sound, feeling the warm breeze and inhaling the now-familiar smell of his skin.

I spent that summer in a dream. It would have been impossible for any girl to not fall in love. I remember my smile when I was aboard the Steve. I remember how pure and real it was. When I look at photos from that time in my life, I nearly don't recognize myself. I'm a naturally happy person, but while I was on that ship, my smile radiated such bliss.

But as it is with all dreams, you have to wake up eventually, and I awoke on July 15, 2011 - the day I left the Steve Irwin in Lerwick, on Scotland's Shetland Islands, and flew home.

I had waited until the night before to book my ticket. I sat alone in James's cabin on my laptop and began to cry the minute I hit the "book flight" button. I sat there with silent tears raging down my face and wondered how I was going to survive this. I hadn't yet become as accustomed to leaving as I am now.

James opened his cabin door and I looked up at him with wet eyelashes. My husband used to leave the room or turn up the car stereo when I would cry; James crossed the small cabin in two steps and had me wrapped up in his arms whispering into my hair.

The next morning, I tried so hard not to cry when I told him goodbye. I've never liked to cry, especially in front of others. I kept the tears in and buried my face in his neck as he hugged me on the dock, his spicy man smell embedding itself in the far reaches of my memory. It still stops my heart when I'm in public and walk past a man with that same smell; it still makes my heart hurt with the memories of the love I used to have for James.

***

On the flight from Scotland, it was all I could do to contain the liquid pain that was threatening to overflow my eyes at any moment. I gazed out the window at the land far below and recapped in my mind all the wonderful friends and memories I had made aboard the Steve Irwin.

I landed in London, knowing that I needed a few days to myself before heading home, and as with every time I've visited that city, it was absolutely pouring down rain. But it matched my mood. I put in my headphones, pulled the hood of my rain jacket up, and walked. For four days, I aimlessly walked, 11 hours the first day, while the rain camouflaged my tears and cleansed me of the heaviness inside my heart, preparing me to go home to the States, to face my parents, with whom I would be living temporarily, and to pretend that I hadn't just experienced a massive personal transformation.

Months would pass before James and I would see each other again. In October 2011, he came to visit me in the States for three weeks. We drove to Vegas to meet up with Steve Irwin crewmates. On the drive, we stopped at a roadside lake to escape the blazing Nevada heat. As I came out of the outhouse, James was standing knee-deep in the water, his hands linked behind his head, gazing out across the lake…butt ass naked. With families eating lunch at nearby picnic tables. I doubled over with laughter, trying to tell him through gasps of breath that he should probably put his clothes on before someone called the cops. Nudity in Australia is not the big deal it is in the States.

We drove to Seattle and Bellingham and he met my friends. We putted around the San Juan Islands aboard my friend's boat and stayed at another crewmates vacation cabin on Whidbey Island. It was bliss, but it was also reality. One I don't think either of us was ready for.

***

In November of 2011, he broke things off with me via email while he was aboard the Steve in Antarctica and I was on the Great Barrier Reef in Australia. I was crushed, and although he wanted to remain friends, I couldn't. There was too much healing I needed to do, and I couldn't be friends with him and pretend that I didn't love him, so I asked him to stop emailing me. He respected my request.

We resumed contact in February of 2012 when he emailed to inform me that the Steve was coming home to Melbourne, Australia after the conclusion of their Antarctic season and he wanted to see me.

I had recently moved to Melbourne and had started casually dating someone else. With the news of the ship's arrival home, and James's cryptic message about having lots of time to think and wanting to see me, I broke things off with the guy I was seeing and met the ship on the dock when it arrived home on March 7, 2012.

As it came into dock, James stood upon her starboard bow and threw me the heaving line.

***

We went right back to how we were; walking the streets of Melbourne, frequenting dark dive bars, reading aloud to each other in local bookshops. I fell in love all over again. I was so angry with him for that.

I had been offered a position in Amsterdam with a startup marine conservation organization and was meant to fly out in a few days. I knew that now was the time when I finally had to give voice to my feelings. I was beyond prepared to sacrifice it all and make a life with him, something I wasn't willing to do even for my ex-husband. As we roamed the darkened streets of Melbourne City with our fellow crewmates and friends, I pulled James aside and proceeded to bare my soul, to offer him my beating heart, and all the love I could possibly give to another person.

That one moment of distraction came at the wrong time; that one moment when I turned my back for an instant because someone called my name. The moment after I had given voice to my true feelings, yet the moment before James had responded. It's so surreal, so un-fucking-real, that it happened the way it did. That it happened at all.

That moment, the small moment in between two pivotal moments, when my back was turned, James got into a cab, and drove away. I turned in time to see him leaning out the passenger window, staring at me, his eyes locked on mine as the cab turned the corner, and then he was gone. Gone. He was simply gone. And I was left standing there on the streets of a foreign city, alone, still loving him, but getting the message loud and fucking clear that he absolutely did not love me.

Only once since then have I made the mistake of being the first one to say I love you. That blew up in my face as well. You can believe that I will never again confess my love, no matter how deep my emotions for that person, until he says it to me first.

***

There were no emails after that fateful night. No text messages. No phone calls. I didn't want an explanation. His actions were explanation enough.

It took me years to even begin to move past the crushing, suffocating, numbing pain that his lack of love had caused me. I spent so many nights sobbing myself to sleep, even years later; tears mixed with the pain of losing him and the burning anger of being the girl who cries herself to sleep over a man. I had tried in every way, shape and form to move on, to get over it, but I simply couldn't. I was too afraid to date someone else, and when I finally did end up dating someone three years later, I realized how extremely unfair it was to that person because I couldn't love him the way he wanted to be loved, because I still loved someone else too much.

It wasn't until the fall of 2015, after I had broken up with my boyfriend and decided to solo road trip from Seattle to Florida that I finally began to move on, for whatever reason. I think I was just exhausted. All I wanted was to forget about James, while still cherishing him. My feelings had finally gone from *in love*, to simply affection for a dear friend, and I will forever consider the friendship we now share to be an abundant blessing in my life.

Now that I'm on the other side of it, I realize with utter clarity just how unnecessary my pain was, and how I had pathetically misplaced my precious emotions for so many years. That's not to imply that he was unworthy of my love, but my torturous pining for him was never going to change anything from his perspective. But it changed me; he changed me. Loving him altered who I am and how I have loved since him. The way I loved him, what I felt we shared, was the most mature of emotions I've ever experienced, yet, until very recently, it was also the closest I had ever come to letting go and loving with full abandon.

However, our accounts of what we shared may differ due to the fact that I never expressed my true feelings to him until it was too late, and then, the brutal reality that it was deeper and more meaningful for me than it was for him was a hard slap in the face. I loved him from the beginning. He didn't love me at all. It was that simple. And it was that painful.

But like all the other heart-shattering events in my life, I embraced the hurt, I learned deeply from it, and I moved on as a stronger and wiser woman because of it. All these years later, it still makes me a little bit sad every time I wear the wooden heart necklace he mailed me from Scotland. When I hear his name or find myself someplace we once visited together it still stings a bit, but it also makes me smile with fond memories.

***

Australia was meant to be my saving grace; my grand escape, my new start. It turned out, however, to be one of the most challenging and miserable times I've ever faced.

Almost immediately after landing in Melbourne I began to feel weighed down by depression and a deep sorrow. I felt so lost it was nearly debilitating; I had no idea what I was doing with myself. I didn't know which direction I wanted my life to go, or how to take the first steps to pull myself out of that black hole. Fortunately, the friends I had (and still have) in Australia served as my own personal shining beacons, lighting the way to better days. My life in Australia felt like a tragedy, one I didn't share with many people, but were it not for those few people, it would have been so much harder.

My time spent living in Airlie Beach, in north Queensland in the Whitsunday Islands, near the Great Barrier Reef, was devastatingly beautiful. When I look back on that harrowing time, I truly believe it was then that I actually found myself. I spent three months there, so alone, when my life was at the pinnacle of its fuckedness, sequestering myself in my tiny hotel room, drowning my sorrows with alcohol. After many years of sobriety, Airlie Beach was the first time I had fallen off the wagon. And not only did I fall, all the judges number cards read 10 as I did a swan dive into the bottom of a whiskey barrel. Damn, did I drink. But I did it alone, and without admitting it to any of my friends (until later, when I was back in Melbourne and fessed up to Georgia), and I did it while lying on my bed sobbing the days and nights away. I could have left Airlie Beach at any time and gone back to Melbourne where I had friends who cared about me, but I nearly violently felt that I was meant to embrace the havoc; to once and for all face head on the destruction of my life instead of running from it, like I was so good at doing.

It was a brutal and lonely time. There was a tiny baby gecko that lived on the ceiling of my bathroom; he became my friend, and my lifeline. He would let go several of his little chirps when I would come home from work, and then we would spend the evenings with me sitting on the cool tile of the bathroom floor, drinking my weight in booze, and sobbing to this gecko about how tragic my life was.

This went on for weeks, until one afternoon, I came home, and the gecko was gone. I cried and cried and drank while lying on the bathroom floor and felt more abandoned than ever before. I couldn't even make things work out with a gecko - no fucking wonder I couldn't hang on to a man.

I think back to that afternoon now and realize how ridiculous it sounds to be so utterly broken up over a gecko, but then I remember how utterly broken I actually was, how completely alone I was. Eventually, I discovered that the gecko had moved to the ceiling of the bedroom and all was right with the world again.

In mid-February 2012, I decided that enough was enough. I sobered up, dried my salty tears, and moved back to Melbourne to be with friends. I spent two more months in Melbourne. I moved in with my dear friend Greg and began casually dating a guy named Aaron.

Aaron and I shared many adventures in our short time together. I would cling to him as we sped down the winding roads of outer Melbourne on his motorcycle and then sit by the water and talk. We danced on rooftops and kissed in dark corners. I think perhaps my favorite memory of Aaron is the night we had dinner in St. Kilda, the beachside neighborhood of Melbourne, and ended up climbing a fence and running down the Grand Prix track.

As we stood looking up at the tall chain-link fence debating about how illegal it would be to climb it, I kicked off my high heels, tossed them over the fence and began to climb. Once our feet hit the other side, I scooped up my shoes and we began running and laughing down the middle of the track. Aaron and I always seemed to have so much fun together, and I love that we're still close friends to this day, even though we live in different hemispheres.

But I was done with Australia. After five months in that country, in which I handed my heart to another person only to have it violently rejected, I moved to Amsterdam.

James and Liberty aboard the Steve Irwin in Barcelona, Spain

Liberty selling merchandise on the Steve Irwin in Barcelona

Liberty and crewmate, Cameron, chipping rust on the Steve Irwin in Barcelona. Vessel Brigitte Bardot in background

Liberty and actress Michelle Rodriguez in Cannes, France

Some of the Steve Irwin crew. Photo by Liberty

Sailing the Strait of Gibraltar

Liberty working on deck of the Steve Irwin after weeks at sea

Liberty and Sea Shepherd founder, Paul Watson

Liberty and the M/Y Steve Irwin. Toulon, France

Actress Michelle Rodriguez jumps from the bow of the Steve Irwin
while Paul Watson looks on. Photo by Liberty

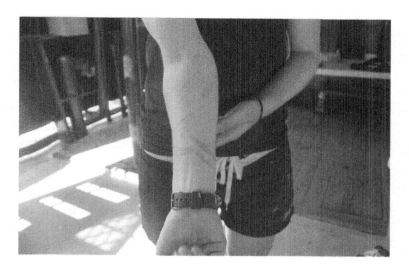

Liberty's arm with jelly stings, nearly three weeks after it happened

Steve Irwin crew members play a game on the aft deck. Photo by Liberty

Chapter Three

"And why do you want to suffer? What are you trying to prove?"
Floater

I grew up with the trees and the raging creek on a 350-acre ranch nestled in Southern Oregon's Rogue Valley, a hot dry bowl of brown landscape in the summer and a cold, sloppy geographic pinpoint in the winter.

Snow fell, and with it came sledding down the hill behind the elementary school and making snow angels in the back field with my best friend, a Native American boy from down the street.

Summers brought oppression in the form of muggy heat and hair-raising thunder storms that turned the sky orange and electrified every ounce of my being. My companions were my big brother, my cousin, and my neighbor; a girlhood filled with boys who taught me to behave like them.

Stripping down to our underwear and jumping from the bridge into Evan's Creek, my fear of heights was a secret embarrassment that I hid from the boys. Despite the apprehension weighing on my tiny body, I swallowed that fear and leapt from the concrete pillars, plunging into the cold and muddy waters below; not unlike how I would eventually live my adult life.

We lazily floated the wide creek on inner tubes and foam boogie boards, even when our mothers told us not to, their well-meaning intentions unable to keep us from leaving the house in the morning and exploring until well after sunset.

We played hide-and-seek in the muggy darkness of summer nights with large bands of neighbor kids, and hundreds of acres at our disposal. We called these games Rambo Parties, and as we aged, they came to include black face paint, camouflage clothing, and cartons of eggs, for this was the era of Red Dawn, and we all wanted to be Wolverines.

Though I had any number of cousins, neighbors and siblings to occupy my time, I remember myself as a lonely child, preferring to be in the forest where I would spend hours alone with my beloved dog by my side, discovering the flora and fauna of the Pacific Northwest; finding small mountain streams with mossy banks to sit upon, buried deep in the furthest corners of the Martin family ranch, while I dreamed of all the wonderful and amazing things I would accomplish as an adult.

In the woods, I had my favorite spots. My mother would trek out to them sometimes to bring me snacks, bananas and apples and little boxes of raisins, knowing that my daydreaming was more important to me than coming home to eat lunch. I didn't realize until I was older how fortunate I was to have a mom who encouraged my wildness and seemed never to doubt my ability to achieve the imaginative things I proclaimed I would someday become – a dolphin trainer, an astronaut, a world traveler.

***

Even though I had been raised within the sheltering bows of the evergreens, it was the sea that called to me. I seemed to have been born with a fiery desperation within me to be a warrior for the ocean; the vast blue world that continues to fascinate me as an adult. My longing to protect the sea was so strong that it was nearly a physical hurt; a desire so deep and overwhelming that my little girl body seemed too meager to contain it. My passion consumed me, and that passion - that desire, and that longing, are things that have never left me, nor diminished with time.

Ever present, living just down the driveway on the other side of the ranch, were my Grandma and Grandpa Martin, my mother's parents and original owners of the J Diamond L Ranch on which I was raised (the J is for James, the L for Lottie, the Diamond for the wedding ring my grandma wore).

My grandfather, embracing our Native American heritage wholeheartedly, descendants of the famed Chief Joseph of the Nez Perce Tribe, hand-built a teepee on the property. He and my Grandma were pillars of the community, and some of the first residents of the tiny community of Wimer, Oregon, an unincorporated area outside the town of Rogue River, purchasing the ranch in 1937.

Having been on the Rogue Valley School Board for nearly 40 years and driving the school bus for many years (my grandmother was the school cook for 10 years), after retiring, my grandfather could never fully separate himself from his love of enriching a child's life. Busloads of students would come from schools around the valley to listen to him regale them with Native tales while they huddled inside the teepee and passed the sage smudge-stick in a circle. The tails of road kill animals and hides he had tanned himself adorned the walls of the teepee, along with strings of beads that my siblings and cousins and I had made for him over the years.

I learned the hard way to never tell my grandpa when I spotted road kill. Waiting for the bus one bitter winter morning when I was about nine, I discovered a dead coyote frozen to the asphalt. I ran up to my grandparents' little white house that sits just off the road and told my grandpa about my find. He handed me a shovel.

As the school bus full of my peers rounded Martin's Corner, the large S curve in front of my grandparents' house, there I was in the middle of the icy road with the shovel in my tiny frigid hands, my pigtails bouncing with the effort of prying the dead coyote off the street, so my grandpa could tan its hide.

My grandfather was the most kind and gentle man with the patience of a saint, yet a demeanor that demanded respect in a quiet, stoic way. His humbleness oozed from his sweet eyes and magic seemed to spill from his hands as he gestured throughout the telling of his Native tales and held kids and adults alike in a tangled web of enchantment.

My grandfather's hands are what I remember most about him; the way he would always hook his pinky fingers into the front pockets of his jeans. They were hands that built a ranch, built a good life, raised children and grandchildren, wielded the willow stick when I was in trouble, and turned the pages of National Geographic magazines while I sat on his lap and he showed me pictures of the world. He, and my grandmother, were the brightest shining lights during my childhood.

It was a childhood of carefree youthful bliss...or so it seemed to anyone who didn't know otherwise.

***

I must have been about six years old the last time I saw my biological father. We were visiting him in Grand Junction, Colorado, where he was stationed as a Navy Recruiter.

He was drunk. He was always drunk, it seemed. On a hot day under the Colorado sun, he came home early from work to find me playing with the neighbor kid, a Hispanic girl my age. He had told me I wasn't allowed to play with her.

On the sidewalk out front of our duplex, he lifted me off the ground by my wrist, my toes clutching for solid ground inside my black and white saddle shoes, my dress swishing around my kicking legs. He struck me repeatedly across my entire backside. Sometimes his fist was open. Sometimes it was closed.

I don't remember if I cried aloud, though I'm sure I must have, but I do remember my brother crying as he watched, just a boy, standing helpless in the presence of a shockingly angry man.

My brother and I never looked away from each other while our father hit me, and even at that young age I remember feeling grateful for him; feeling as if I had found a lighthouse in the storm, and I clung to him with my eyes and my heart.

That moment is one of the first memories I have of the deep love I held for my older brother. Even though he couldn't physically stop our dad, his presence provided me with the strength I needed to endure. I've clung to that strength all my life. There is always something to endure, it seems.

The evening progressed into the typical violent ordeal that we had become accustomed to: Dad drank. Dad got angry over insignificant things. Dad beat someone up, usually our mom. The night ended with my mom making the three of us kids walk to the police station with her.

Later, while everyone else sat in the living room of our neighbor's house, Neosporin and Band-Aids littering the coffee table after treating our multitude of cuts from the glass shards of a lamp hurled against the wall, I crawled up onto the counter of the dark kitchen and watched while my father was handcuffed, led across our yard and put into the back of a police car. He spotted me in the window, stopping just before he was pushed down onto the backseat. I still remember the clothes he was wearing, the white shirt revealing the tattoos on his forearms. His face was blank as he held me in his gaze. Even at that age, I recognized the deep anger in his blue eyes; the hatred inside him was tangible from across the yard and through the closed window. Sitting with my bare feet in the kitchen sink and my hands gripping the windowsill, I shuddered with fear.

It was a pivotal moment for my little girl self, one which struck terror into every corner of my body, a fear that returns repeatedly and is triggered without warning. To this day it still takes a conscious effort to not flinch in defense when any man makes sudden movements. When it happens, it makes my eyes burn with hidden tears of shame that I unwillingly harbor this intense fear, even around the kindest of men. For all the times I've been told I'm brave, there are more times of pain and terror that I hide from everyone.

I used to lay awake at night when my father still lived with us on the ranch and stare out the window at the blanket of stars draped over the Southern Oregon sky. I would silently beg, plead, and pray to wake up in the morning as something else (I was only four or five years old; it was usually a cat or a mermaid) so that I wouldn't have to live that traumatic and abusive life any longer.

For all the carefree wonderful times I experienced growing up on the ranch after my father left, the foundation of my formative years was cracked, broken, sunken and missing large pieces. Deep scars of hurt and fear were slashed into me every time my father hit me, every time I watched him hit my mother or my siblings.

As I got older and my father eventually faded from our lives, I sought so many wrong ways to fill that void he had created by his abuse, and then his absence. Though he'd left, part of him was never really gone. Always the sadness held my hand; the demons filled my dreams while I slept. And I still hadn't gotten my wish to be a mermaid. At least, not yet.

***

I can still feel the belt tight around my neck the first time I tried to kill myself, the air straining to reach my lungs while my heart pounded inside my head. I must have been about thirteen years old. The sinking aloneness that enveloped my life left me feeling hollow. I wanted to die, but I was terrified to stop existing.

I had strung the belt up around the rod in my closet, and I remember looking at the bright green carpet while my eyes thudded to the beating of my pulse. I had to hide the bruises on my neck after that, but by then, I had been hiding the scars and the pain all my life.

The second time, it was pills. A combination of Ibuprofen, Tylenol and Midol. I didn't have the courage to take anything stronger, though I could have easily gotten my hands on it, so I swallowed a shocking amount of the generic stuff. That sick feeling in my stomach stayed with me for days. My guilt and sorrow stayed even longer.

The suffocation of life was like a physical pain crushing my soul. Shrouded in darkness, with no hope of light, there were times when I would do anything to feel alive, to feel loved and needed, but I was too afraid to cry out publicly for help. It seemed there was always so much turmoil going on at home that my feelings of despair were insignificant, at least in my own mind. This book is the first most people will hear of my close encounters with suicide.

The cutting began once I realized I would never have the courage to actually kill myself. It was a way to transfer pain; to make it tangible. I couldn't cry, so I bled. I couldn't find words for the horrid things I was feeling inside, and I felt as if I had no one to voice those words to anyway, so I carried my pain on my skin. In a solitary-feeling life full of chaos, confusion and endless abandonment, cutting was something I finally had control over.

I left my scars out in the open; my red wounds taunting those who worried about me. I told myself that I wasn't ashamed; that it was either cutting or suicide and that I had chosen the lesser of two evils. I still have those scars on my arms, a reminder of that desperate and lonely little girl I used to be.

And then I discovered drugs. Suicide was too scary, so I tumbled into a drug-induced oblivion and tried on purpose to die on accident. I'm surprised I didn't die. I should have. The things I was doing are things that no one should have survived. Yet every morning when I awoke, I would cry out in despair that I was being forced to endure another day.

Every girl and woman in this world walks a tight rope created by men, but also created by ourselves and by society. The lack of love from my father instilled within me a desire to be loved, to be wanted, and like so many women, I confused sex with love. My fear of men ran deep, but I figured if I gave them what they wanted, I had no reason to be afraid of them. The feeling of being held safely within a man's arms while he kissed me and told me I was beautiful was as intoxicating as any drug. I craved that closeness; that feeling of importance; that feeling…of love.

Yet when they actually loved me, I ran, because if they loved me, they could hurt me and leave me. But not if I left first. That mentality has grown within me as the years have passed, and it's a mentality that has caused immense damage in my life as an adult. It's always been me that pushes men away; it's always been me that leaves first, and then I wonder why I can't find a man to love me. It's pretty fucked up the way I sabotage myself and my relationships, yet it's something I've only become consciously aware of within the past couple years, and the two times I've tried to change the way I am, to stick around and make a relationship work because I did truly love them, they've walked away from me, and it throws me back into that emotional wasteland of feeling worthless and unwanted and unlovable.

***

My father taught me many things before he finally exited my life for good that night in Colorado. He taught me to be afraid of men, to lash out when angry, to hold grudges, and to let your past dictate your entire existence. And he taught me how to drink.

I was good at the anger, the fear, and the bitterness, but I was exceptionally good at the drinking.

As I moved into my late teenage years, I could hold my own, pounding beers and taking shots with the guys. Putting away a half gallon of Tequila a night, with the help of a few friends, was a normal occurrence. Liquor and beer, mixed with random pills, weed, acid and mushrooms, and whatever else was generously put into my hands was a nightly cocktail. I got myself into trouble more than once on account of my haphazard approach to drug-taking.

But it was the alcohol that beckoned to me from across the room at every party; the alcohol that called my name in the dark of night and made me shake with want during the hours we were apart. It was the alcohol, in any form, that brought out my rage and my hate. Shots of cough syrup in the convenient little plastic cup that comes turned upside down over its lid was my go-to. Even after I was old enough to buy beer, the high alcohol content and accessibility of the cough syrup was just too easy to pass up.

The first boyfriend I ever lived with, when I was 17, would come home from work at night to find me passed out on the floor of our house, empty Nyquil bottles scattered around me like a bad Saturday Night Live skit, while the bottle of muscle relaxers drastically diminished each day as well. Exasperated, he would carry me to bed time and again. I was a fucking train wreck.

I would wake in the mornings and go to high school with a throbbing head and drooping eyes. Each morning was like doing a version of the walk of shame from the bedroom to the front door, the cough syrup and pill bottles left to lie where I had dropped them in a stupor the night before. Also present were signs of the fury that rose from within me while I was intoxicated – smashed dishes in the kitchen sink, chairs overturned, and once, even an axe through the living room wall. This was what I had become – a violent, fucked up person with absolutely no respect for anyone else and a complete disregard for life. And I was only a senior in High School.

I went to school with bottles of cough syrup and No-Doz in my backpack and would chase one with the other all day long in class. Despite how far gone I seemed to be, I still clung to a determination to graduate. I don't know why; it would have been so easy to drop out since I wasn't living with my parents any longer and had a job as a prep cook at a local restaurant. Maybe it was the only thing I had in my life at that point that was worth hanging on to.

The anger that took control when I was drunk, the bitter rage of a lifetime of bullshit that gripped me tightly, dangled me from its strings like a joke of a puppet. One drink in, and the white-hot rage would begin to bubble up from the depths to which I had banished it. I had no self control while I was drunk, and a bottomless pit of hatred for being alive. I would lash out at anything and anyone in my path, with no regard.

My father's choice to abuse me and then abandon me was something that left me devastatingly broken. But it also left me too prideful to admit how shattered I was, so I learned to pretend - to pretend that I didn't care, that it didn't matter, that it didn't affect me. I had a gaping hole inside of me that I attempted to fill with booze and pills and guys; the strong façade I portrayed was a shield of armor against how destroyed I felt.

I never wanted to believe I was a girl with 'daddy issues', yet it became apparent in nearly all of my romantic relationships that I was 'that girl'. I was afraid of men, I was afraid to be hurt again, to be walked out on the way my father had walked out on me (years later, a therapist would proclaim that I held the most intense fear of abandonment he had ever witnessed), so I portrayed myself as indifferent, while inside I was searing with a storm of bottled emotions. I cared too much, I felt too deeply and yet I was stuck in that pretending mode that I had learned as a young girl; pretending I was tough, that I didn't need anyone, especially not a man, and that I wasn't hurt or bothered by all the fucked up things men had done to me.

I realize now that I enabled them to do those hurtful things because I feigned indifference. Why wouldn't they take advantage if I pretended not to care that they had gotten someone else pregnant and then stolen money from me to pay for the abortion? And all this I learned from my sister, who had overheard it at the hair salon, of all gossipy places. I pretended I didn't care in public, and then would sit in my car alone in the mountains crying, drinking, taking pills and slashing my skin open with the little pocket knife on my keychain. Again...a fucking train wreck.

Despite the horrid things my father had done when I was a child, I still longed to meet him, to see his face, to hear his voice. It was the one thing I wanted most for nearly thirty years, more than finding a good man who would treat me right, more than having money, more than traveling the world. I wanted to lay my eyes upon the man who had paved the way to me being the broken person I had become.

Chapter Four

"Crawling home from some saloon, and all my strings are out of tune.
No one's around to break my fall" Floater

I landed at Schipol airport in Holland on April 2, 2012, a cold and crisp spring morning. My life had taken so many twists and turns in the past two years, and I never imagined that I would be standing at Central Station in Amsterdam, waiting for a girl with whom I had gone all through school in tiny Rogue River, Oregon.

I was meant to meet her at the train station before she went off to work in Haarlem so she could give me the key to her apartment. I was going to be staying with her for a bit until I could move into the staff house for the non-profit I had come to work with. We hadn't seen each other in 18 years. She had been living in Amsterdam for about a year, Los Angeles before that.

Embracing at the train station made the years disappear and I was thrilled to see her beautiful face, and to be far away from Australia. She handed over the key before boarding the train to Haarlem, and I set about dragging my luggage through winding alleys and over canal bridges to her apartment, right on the banks of the Amstel River.

I promptly climbed into the bathtub while her dog and cat wondered who the hell I was, and soaked away the grime of travel and the dirt of life.

For the next few weeks, Alethia and I had the most fun. To be in the presence of such a strong and amazing woman was beyond healing. We shared our past hurts and our future hopes and spent evenings dressing up and going to music.

As we reminisced one night, Alethia shared with me a memory of when I was five and she was seven and I showed her how to make cinnamon toast. How wild is life? Who would have thought that two Wimer, Oregon girls would be catching up as women living as expats in Amsterdam?

Amsterdam has the most incredible live music scene, and I found it thrilling to be sharing space with someone who adored music as much as I did.

I can imagine that being in the heart of a crowded concert is like being in the womb; the suffocating press on all sides of your body, the warmth of life surrounding you (though I'm sure the womb is sans the smell of sweaty bodies), the underwater muffle of a thousand sounds colliding and, of course, the waiting; waiting for the moment when something big happens, when it all begins. A feeling of suspension always encompasses me while I'm photographing a show. The outside world fades away, the past recedes, the future doesn't exist yet, and all that truly matters is the moment I'm in.

Music, and live music in particular, has always been a chosen method of escape for me, and I crave those few hours when the tunes fill my soul and my body and cleanse my mind of all the stresses of life. Music serves another purpose for me as well; a connection to someone I loved and lost.

One of the first live shows I went to as an early teen was for a band that my brother was good friends with. My brother was at that show, and he acknowledged me, the nerdy little sister, in front of his friends. Remember that feeling when you were young with a massive crush, and then that person talked to you...in public? That was akin to this moment at the concert. My brother was my idol, and music was a passion we shared.

After his death when I was 16, music and concerts were part of my escape. But more than that, they were my connection to the brother I had lost. It never ceases to amaze me how powerful music can be.

I once photographed an Ellie Goulding show in Seattle. Her album, Halcyon, was born of the pain from her very difficult breakup with her boyfriend. During the show, she made a comment that resonated strongly with me. She talked of the pain that accompanies the departure of a relationship, but that eventually you reach a point of acceptance, and then one day, you realize that you're no longer in love with that person, no longer in pain over losing that person and that you're finally happy, not because you've found someone new, but because you've found YOU.

That hit home with me, because I had lived through this entire process so many times: I'd loved, I'd lost, it hurt like a son of a bitch, and it took a long time, but eventually, it didn't hurt anymore, and I realized that I was happy again; happy because of me, happy with me. And through it all, through the pain and the happiness, music has been my ever-faithful companion.

***

Every morning in Amsterdam, I would ride my bike to work on the other side of the city and spend my days in meetings that consisted of aimlessly wandering the streets of Amsterdam while brainstorming ways to combat the world-wide issue of over-fishing.

While Amsterdam was in the grips of the most brutal cold snap I think I've ever experienced, my heart was warming (it was probably all the bike riding) and my smile was returning. Amsterdam is a city that oozes history and I adored every second of my time there. I find now that it's the one place my heart still aches for.

After the pain of Australia and the happiness of Amsterdam, and two years overseas, home began to beckon to me from across the ocean. I was tired. I was still broken, yet no longer shattered. I was exhausted and still had no idea which direction I was going in life. But more pressing was the fact that I had no money. My savings was gone, my credit cards were maxed, and I was still a volunteer. As much as I longed to, I simply couldn't stay on in Amsterdam with no money, and no visa to work. It was time to go home. Home to Bellingham, Washington. BellingHOME, as the locals lovingly refer to it.

After two months in Amsterdam, I boarded a plane to Seattle.

No one ever told me how difficult it would be to come home after living overseas. No one warned me that connecting with old friends, with family, with people in general, would be harder than ever before. I've always felt out of place and alone, but there was something different about this. This was crushing; nearly debilitating. This made me gaze into nothingness while the world revolved around me.

I had never heard of Reverse Culture Shock until my mom gave me a Lonely Planet travel book about volunteering internationally. While flipping through the book hoping to see amazing photos of exotic destinations, I came upon a chapter about this very serious, very common, and yet very unknown condition. What I read changed everything.

After my years living abroad, I had hit a wall. I was emotionally and financially drained. I was tired of sleeping on the couches of strangers, tired of saying goodbye to people I had come to love so deeply in such a short amount of time. I was tired of being alone, yet always surrounded by people. So, I went home to Bellingham, a small coastal community 90 miles north of Seattle, and like with any honeymoon phase, I was blissfully in love with simply being home.

Time went by and I realized, though I initially ignored it, that I was struggling to connect with the people I knew there, the people I had always known there, the people who had known me before I was the near-famous, globe-trotting, marine conservationist nomad. How do you explain what you've experienced to someone who hasn't had the same, or similar, experience? You don't. You can't. How do you convey the wonders of Italian history or the harrowing sorrow of seeing Libyan refugees on derelict rafts in the middle of the ocean? How do you put into words the paralyzing horror of standing at the Cove watching the ocean turn red with dolphin blood? You don't. You can't. You keep it inside and you hide the fact that you hear dolphins crying inside your heart and mind every second of every day. You become addicted to sleeping pills to keep the nightmares at bay. And you feel so very alone, all the time.

I learned to hide the crushing, life-sucking feelings that were happening inside me. Everything in my life at home was so frustratingly unfamiliar. I forgot which side of the road to drive on. I forgot which currency was in my wallet. I forgot if I was supposed to greet someone with a handshake, a hug, a kiss on the cheek, or a bow. Things that used to be so easy, so familiar, were now monumental mountains that shadowed my life.

Reverse Culture Shock is very real, and all the research I had done showed that it's more devastating than Culture Shock, because you come home to a place you loved, to the people you loved, and you realize that everything has changed for you, but not for them. You've changed.

My time overseas had reprogrammed my entire being; my soul had been awakened by the experiences I had, and it was now impossible to be satisfied with my bi-weekly paycheck, my sports-shifting Subaru, and my apartment overlooking downtown. My tolerance for mindless submission to the American Dream was now non-existent. That first year being home was a challenge indeed. Knowing – truly knowing – that there was a wide, magical world out there waiting to reveal its exciting secrets and yet feeling trapped, was enough to drive me nearly mad. The only thing that kept me going was the hope that one day I'd be released back into the wild. I hung on to that hope for dear life.

I escaped my struggles with an outlet that had always been available to me – music. I immersed myself in the local music scene, eventually starting a company that managed, promoted, and photographed bands.

Black Anchor Productions kept me from drowning. I was back to working full-time as a photographer, and ran Black Anchor in my off-time, though it became a time-consuming hobby. I organized west coast tours for indie bands and booked shows and worked the merch table and hung posters and did whatever else was necessary to help musicians flourish.

It all began by organizing a 10-band music festival a few months after I came home from overseas. I was losing my mind with being in one spot, and needed an outlet. So I put on a music festival in a parking lot in Bellingham that was free to the public and showcased local bands from Bellingham and Seattle. I brought in a beer garden and food trucks and a coffee stand and face painters and circus guild performers and handed it all to the public free of charge.

Though the bands didn't get paid, I ended up spending more than a thousand dollars from my own pocket to make it all happen. And it was worth it. The music festival kickstarted my involvement in the west coast indie music scene and before I knew it, I had nearly 40 bands between Victoria, British Columbia and Southern Oregon that I was helping. I spent my days at my photography job glued to my iPhone, and my nights and weekends were spent talking with bands, meeting with bands, planning with bands, and going to shows. And I never got paid one penny. But my payment came in the form of free concert tickets. That was enough for me.

The truth of my travel was that I had been running around the globe desperately seeking a place where I belonged, all the while claiming that I was doing it out of adventure. I've always been good at running away and pretending I'm not crumbling inside.

Though it took me nearly two years, years of rest and normalcy that I desperately needed after my journeys, I finally broke free and immersed myself in the world again.

***

Randomly, in the fall of 2013, after I had left my photography job, I met a girl in Bellingham while I was working as an Animal Control Officer for the Humane Society. She was a chef aboard a small luxury eco-cruise ship in Alaska during the summers. I had responded to her call about a cat trapped under her house. We got to talking about Alaska and the fact that I had crewed aboard the Steve Irwin and had lived in Alaska at two different times in my life. She connected me with the Captain of the boat. In the spring of 2014, I found myself aboard the M/V Liseron, owned and operated by The Boat Company in Poulsbo, Washington, as she sailed north to Alaska.

The Liseron, which means morning glory in French, is a 1952 wooden mine sweeper that served in the French military. She was a gorgeous girl with clean lines and the unique smell of a wooden ship. At 500 tons and 150 feet, she boasted original Cleveland diesels and brass throughout, and she captured my heart the moment I laid eyes upon her.

The Boat Company, and the Liseron, are by far one of the best things to happen in my life. I fell into the company by chance, and five years later, I'm sitting aboard the Liseron as I type this. I've been with The Boat Company longer than I've had any job, and the beginning of each season brings with it excitement to get back to my beautiful old wooden girl.

I began as summer crew in early 2014, serving aboard the Liseron in Southeast Alaska as the Guest Coordinator. Since then, I have been a part of the winter crew, a small group of craftsmen who keep her looking classy, from painting and sanding to varnishing and repairing.

I'm the sole winter liveaboard and spend my nights alone on this big boat, listening to her breathe. I know every creak and groan, every nook and cranny and every quirk. She is one of the greatest loves of my life. She is my beacon in the fog.

Just as with my first glimpse of the Steve Irwin, laying my eyes upon the Liseron made my heart swell with joy. She had been refitted from a mine sweeper to what she is today - a 20 passenger luxury eco-cruise vessel who spends her summers in the waters of Southeast Alaska. She was stunning. And I was going to spend the next six months living and working aboard her. It was an adventure, indeed, an adventure that turned out to be, like most things in my life seem to, a challenging blessing.

It was April 2014 and I had been home in Bellingham for not quite two years when I packed my bags again and headed first to the south, Port Orchard, Washington, and then sailed to the north, Alaska.

We spent several weeks dockside in Port Orchard prepping the Liseron and her sister ship, the Mist Cove, and in early May, we cast off for our northbound voyage. We would spend the next 16 weeks taking passengers on week-long cruises through Southeast Alaska, between Juneau and Sitka, all the while attempting to foster within them a passion to protect Alaska's Tongass National Forest in the Alexander Archipelago.

The hours were long, the work was hard, and living in such close quarters with fellow crewmates was often-times harder. But I loved it. I was on a boat, seeing whales nearly every day, hiking in rainforests with grizzly bears, kayaking fog-enshrouded bays and doing what I do best - making friends with strangers.

At the end of the six month season, I walked away with more money in my bank than I'd ever had before, and again, I went home to Bellingham, to my apartment that I had lived in for years (and had kept while I was away in Alaska) and to my cat, Kamea (which my neighbor was looking after). I was exhausted from the months of hard work and, for now, my wanderlust was satisfied. But I now had thousands of dollars burning a hole in my bank account, so after only two weeks of being home, I boarded a plane to Florida and spent the next three weeks with friends who live in the Tampa area. Back in Bellingham for a week, and then I was off to visit my friends Down Under, this time with my 18 year old nephew in tow. I never thought I'd be going back to Australia...

***

Since my nephew and I were passing through Byron Bay during our time in Australia, I emailed James asking if he wanted to meet for coffee. It had been three years since we'd seen each other, since that disastrous night in Melbourne, and just as long since we'd talked.

He suggested that my nephew, Cole, and I stay at his place on the beach for a few days. We agreed. Cole and James had met before when James came to the States to spend three weeks with me in late 2011.

After landing in Brisbane, renting a car, and driving the several hours to James's house, Cole and I arrived after midnight. James was asleep, but had sent an email directing me to the spare bedroom.

I was awoken early the next morning, darkness still clinging to the Australian sky, to James sitting on the edge of the bed, looking down at me. Clutching my stuffed cat (yes, I slept with a stuffed cat whose name was Orion), wearing earplugs and dead to the world after a long flight and drive, it was not the first impression I wanted to make after so many years apart. But there he was. We hugged, and Lord have mercy, he smelled the same. I hated myself for it, but my heart skipped a few beats.

We spent the next couple of weeks in sunshine-drenched heaven. Cole and I made the 14-hour trek up to Airlie Beach and spent several days lounging at the Airlie Lagoon (a notorious glorified swimming pool in the heart of town, since going into the ocean during "jelly season", which means there's too many deadly jellyfish, is out of the question), catching up with old friends I had made during my three months living there, and cruising on the Derwent Hunter, the beautiful sailboat I used to work aboard. We spent our balmy Australian evenings drinking colorful drinks (non-alcoholic for me) at the backpacker's bars. The drinking age in Australia is 18, so I was able to buy Cole his first-ever legal beer, something every cool aunt should do.

Back near Byron Bay, we spent an entire day on the beach with James at Evan's Head. Cole beach-combed while I read, and James kayaked with wild dolphins. Later, we went to South Golden Beach, across from James's house, and stargazed while the bioluminescence lit up the waves around our bare, sandy feet. Magic has always seemed to follow James, and even after all those years, he still had it. Damn him.

After a perfect day, James and I stayed up talking in the kitchen. As the late hours dawned, we hugged goodnight...and didn't let go. I ended up in his bedroom, knowing very well what was going to happen, but letting it happen anyway. Sleeping next to him was as natural as breathing, and the familiarity of it all was heartbreakingly beautiful. It was also exactly the closure I had needed for so many years.

The next morning, feeling guiltily like the world's worst aunt, I attempted to creep into the room I shared with Cole before he awoke and crawl into my bed, like I had been there all night. I quietly pulled the door to James's bedroom closed behind me and tip-toed into the living room. Cole was sitting on the couch. As I stopped short, busted doing the walk of shame by my 18 year old nephew, Cole looked up at me with a smirk, gave me the man nod, and said "what's up, Aunt Libby?" We both started laughing as I dropped down next to him on the couch. Neither of my nephews have ever called me 'aunt', they have always simply called me 'Libby'.

The days wore on, and Cole got on a plane home to the States. Saying goodbye to him in the Brisbane airport was what I imagine to be the closest thing I've ever felt to being a mother. I worried about him, but knew that I couldn't go with him. I nagged him about watching his bags and not being "that American". I worried he wouldn't find his gate, or his seat, or that his plane would crash. I hugged him goodbye and then found a place to cry. He had been my first travel companion, and while I'm an advocate for solo travel, I realized suddenly just how lonely it can be.

I spent that night in the Brisbane airport and boarded a plane the next day to Auckland, New Zealand. I had planned to fly home with Cole to Oregon and spend the holidays with my family, but as Christmas neared, New Zealand called. I was already in Australia, I figured, I might as well backpack New Zealand. Of course, my mother understood and encouraged me to go. My parents have always been amazingly supportive of my roaming, and for that I will be eternally grateful.

After spending a day wandering Auckland, I jumped a bus to the town of Thames on the Coromandel Peninsula and met up with an old Sea Shepherd buddy, Pete Bethune.

Drinking cider at The Junction Hotel on a sunny evening, Pete and I caught up on life, marine conservation, and Sea Shepherd drama, of which there seemed to be no shortage. Pete, being the wise Kiwi bloke he is, pointed out that one of the greatest things to come out of Sea Shepherd was the multitude of different great conservation groups that have been formed by scorned Sea Sheep (our nickname for Sea Shepherd volunteers). How true.

I bussed it back to Auckland, and boarded a plane to Wellington and stepped out into the great and windy city that is so legendary. Windy Wellington, indeed.

A four hour ferry ride dropped me in Pickton, on the northern tip of the southern island of New Zealand. I spent New Year's Eve 2014 asleep in a hostel, surrounded by empty bunks. I awoke on January 1, 2015 to beds occupied by passed-out-drunk co-ed backpackers. I quickly showered, my first in many days, grabbed my REI backpack, and started walking the abandoned early-morning streets. I found a coffee shop and spent my morning sipping a flat white (a very popular espresso drink in New Zealand and Australia) and eating a peaceful solo breakfast at the water's edge. It was a beautifully sad way to welcome the New Year.

After another bus ride, the next four days consisted of exploring the adorable town of Nelson and kayaking the waters of Abel Tasman National Park.

Though I'm not a religious person by any means, when traveling, I tend to seek out churches and cathedrals. The history and quiet sanctity appeals to the spiritual side of me, and I found just such a cathedral in Nelson, in the heart of town.

I visited the church many times, and spent hours sitting in contemplation and lighting candles for my brother and other lost loved ones. On an early morning visit, the hushed pews revealed to me the sound of crying. I looked over and watched a young girl slide from the pew onto her knees, her hands clasped in prayer, her eyes shut tight. She silently mouthed her pleas to God while salty rivers flooded her cheeks. My heart broke, because I knew exactly how she felt. And my heart broke, because she had the courage to cry out to some higher power and beg for help, and I didn't.

My disdain for God and religion, though I was currently sitting in a church, was extraordinary. I had spent a lifetime having Christianity forced down my throat, and as an adult I chose to vehemently oppose such beliefs. I frequented churches during my travels simply for the history.

Upon leaving Nelson, I embarked on a two-day bus ride, during which my seatmate, who happened to be a very attractive younger guy, slept most of the ride with his head on my shoulder, but I let him, because, like I said, he was insanely sexy.

I arrived in Christchurch weary and smelly, and was greeted by the smiling faces of my old bosses from Paradise Bay in Australia, on the Whitsunday Islands, Steve and Rosie. Steve is American, Rosie is a Kiwi, and after a long stint in Australia, they were back in Christchurch managing a hotel. It felt like a lifetime since I had seen them. After catching up on the back porch of the hotel, they showed me to my room for the next week. I had never been so grateful for a bathtub in all my life.

Aaron, the Australian guy I had been casually seeing in Melbourne, was now also living in Christchurch, and after collecting me from the hotel he and I had dinner and a proper catch-up and then met his girlfriend (also an American) for drinks at the local pub. Two days later he came calling at the hotel again and took me driving up into Arthur's Pass. We stopped and picked up a hitchhiker along the way, a young Frenchman named Remi with whom we made fast friends.

We spent the day hiking to Devil's Punchbowl Falls, drinking the pristine water straight from the source, and napping upon warm boulders. It was the most beautiful day, and one that I will remember for a long time to come.

At the end of the day, we stopped and grabbed a pizza and sat in the park eating right out of the box. He then dropped me at the hotel and I flew back to Australia early the next morning, and then home to the States a few days later.

That trip was a beautiful way to dispel my negative feelings toward Australia. Catching up with old friends and showing my nephew around made me see the country in a new light, and while I don't despise it as much as I used to, Australia will forever be a place I feel somewhat hostile towards. That time in Australia was also the catalyst I needed to once and for all put my feelings for James behind me. I was exhausted from loving him. The friendship we share to this day is a peaceful reminder for me of how amazing and unpredictable life is.

Like so many times before, I headed home to Bellingham. Yet as is common with me, after about two months, I was restless again, and ready for a new adventure. I decided to give up my amazing little apartment overlooking downtown and move onto a sailboat in Friday Harbor, San Juan Island. The San Juan's, northwest of Seattle, are gorgeous islands that float peacefully in Puget Sound, bordered by Washington's mainland and Canada's Vancouver Island. I had spent a good bit of time in the islands due to Sea Shepherd being headquartered there and had several friends who lived there. I got a kayak guiding job, packed my things into storage in Bellingham and Kamea (my cat) and I moved aboard the Colina, a 46' Cal sailboat docked at Shipyard Cove Marina on the outskirts of the town of Friday Harbor. I had no idea how my life was about to change.

Liberty and Alethia in Amsterdam

Liberty hitching a ride, Dutch style

A music festival in Haarlem with the girls

Riding bikes in Holland

Liberty kayaks in Southeast Alaska near the M/V Liseron

Liberty and the Liseron

Liberty at Dawes Glacier in Southeast Alaska

Hiking Red Bluff in Southeast Alaska

Liberty and Cole at SeaTac airport, heading to Australia

Cole and James haul the kayak across the beach at Evan's Head

Airlie Beach, Australia

A storm rolls in over South Golden Beach

Liberty and Pete Bethune in Thames, New Zealand

Steve and Rosie

The Auckland Sky Tower

Aaron naps on a warm boulder at Devils Punchbowl Falls

Chapter Five

"This world has gone and drug us along. Nothing's the same, and it will never be again" Floater

I couldn't see her, but I could hear her, and the sound of my mother, crumpled on the kitchen floor, clutching the telephone to her chest and sobbing over and over, "I don't know how to handle this", is something that breaks my heart to this very day, the heavy sickening feeling never diminishing despite the passing of years.

My brother, Bern, was murdered when I was 16 years old. My lighthouse, my rock, my source of strength, my replacement father, and my best friend. Murdered. It's hard enough being a girl that age without throwing homicide into the hormonal mix.

Shot in the face numerous times by friends on his 21st birthday because of marijuana and dumped over an embankment on a logging road, my brother's body was left to the elements, decomposing for nearly two months before he was found, before we even knew that he was dead. It was quite literally the moment that shaped who I am as I sit here today writing this. I've struggled for the past 20 years since his death in 1997 to write this book, to account it all on paper in the hopes that my words will somehow help another young girl out there who is caught in the middle of feeling alone, lonely, lost, and forgotten. I wasn't ready until now to write it, and I've decided to leave a good portion of the gruesome details of his death out of this book. I could never attempt to fully put into words the feelings of having your older, and only, brother murdered by his friends.

The phone call that changed my family forever came in the early morning hours of December 3, 1997 from the Josephine County Coroner confirming the identity of my brother's body, and it was, at the same time, the beginning, and the end for me.

It was the beginning of a chaotic, out of control time that also happened to serve as one of the most liberating times in my life. There's something to be said for letting go; for just living and being, for simply existing and allowing life to happen to you. There's something to be said for just not giving a fuck anymore.

I was the last person in my family to see Bern alive. The day before he died, the day before his birthday, I was driving down Queen's Branch Road in Wimer with friends. We passed Bern and his friend, Mike, walking up Queen's Branch. I asked my friend to pull over so I could wish Bern an early happy birthday. I didn't see him too often those days.

I stood on the side of the road with Bern and Mike, making awkward small talk, and then hugged Mike. As I leaned in to hug my brother, I was overcome with a feeling of not wanting to embarrass him, so I pulled away from the hug at the last minute, instead touching the pin on his jacket collar and saying it was cool. I looked up into his brown eyes and said "well, if I don't see you again, happy birthday." And then I walked away and got into the car. Those last words to him haunt me still, and when I really think about my life and the things I could potentially regret, that day is what comes to mind first. I deeply and painfully regret not hugging my brother.

Months later, I went to the police station with my parents when they collected Bern's effects. The three of us sat in the car in the parking lot, my mom clinging to the brown paper sack the police had given her. She cried as she held it, none of us saying anything. She couldn't open it, so she handed the bag to me in the backseat.

As I opened the top and peered in, I remember thinking that the stench coming from inside smelled like money. I pulled a paper towel from the bag and unwrapped what was inside. It was the pin from his jacket collar; the one I had touched the last time I saw him. The wings of the eagle had turned green from the months his body had spent exposed to the elements.

Twenty years later, my mom gave me that pin for my 36th birthday. That pin, along with a red heart key chain that Bern gave me for my 16th birthday, and a few bullet casings collected from where he died on Sykes Creek Road are the only tangible items I have left of the brother I so deeply adored, idolized, and loved.

Many years prior to the onslaught of my drug and alcohol abuse, somehow, I had fallen, even at that young age, into the role of the responsible one; I was so cautious about everything, so organized and always prepared, yet I was utterly lost as to who I truly was and who I wanted to become. The only things I've ever been certain about in life are the ocean and music and the undying love I possess for both.

That phone call from the coroner was my moment of truth, and I reached out and viciously grabbed it with both hands.

It was 3am, a school night for me, then a junior in high school, and my family sat gathered in our living room, silent as stone figures, waiting for the call from the coroner; waiting to see if the body on his cold, metal table was my brother.

No one talked. No one ate, though so much food cluttered the kitchen counter. The atmosphere was crushingly heavy with a combination of awkwardness, fear and anger. How like my brother to put us through this; to make us worry and wonder. His anger, an anger that ruled our household and dominated everything, just like our fathers had, was a force to be reckoned with.

Twice in the months leading up to his disappearance I had the misfortune of being home with him and our stepdad when they fought. As he came down off drugs, my brother would rage and attack the man who was more of a dad to us than our biological father ever had been. With his lanky 6'5" frame, his long jet-black hair pulled back with a bandana, a hefty swag chain at his hip, and tie-dyed Grateful Dead shirts, Bern was an intimidating sight, even when he wasn't in a drug-induced hysteria. The fear I experienced during his frequent moments of savage anger was unparalleled, and I was devastated that I had come to fear him, the only man I had ever truly loved at that point in my life. And I hated him for making me afraid of him.

He would scream at our stepdad while he smashed everything he could get his hands on, and when the two of them came to blows, I would crawl into the depths of my bedroom closet, rock back and forth with my hands over my ears, and beg whatever God was listening for our stepdad to survive this round.

The last time they fought, just weeks before Bern died, I barricaded myself in my bedroom, frantically pushing my dresser in front of my door and huddling into the dark corner of my closet as I listened to them destroy each other. I put in my headphones and cried. The urge to scream, to release the built-up rage within me was so overwhelming at times I thought that alone would surely kill me. How was this my life?! And then the gun shots made me rip my headphones out. Silence. Two gun shots, and then silence. Nothing. I must have sat there for an eternity, my breath held, salty tears drying on my face, 16 years old, hiding in a closet.

Eventually finding the courage to open my bedroom door, I was immediately met with the sight of bloody walls. Fingers of violent red smeared across the stark white walls, all the way down the hallway. I stopped to flick on the bathroom light, and brought my left hand away doused in someone else's blood. The stopper had been pulled and the bathroom sink was half full of the dark red liquid.

As I made my way into the kitchen, broken glass crunched under my ever-present combat boots. It was like a war zone. Everything was broken, chairs were upturned, blood everywhere. My dad was gone, his truck no longer in the driveway. That's when the fury inside of me boiled up from the depths and exploded. That's when I found my strength.

I used my Dr. Marten's boots to kick open my brother's bedroom door like the bad ass I definitely wasn't and found him lying on his back on the floor, holding a towel to his nose. Never before, and never since, have I screamed at someone the way I screamed at him that day.

My hatred for him and how he was destroying our family had finally won out over my fear of him.

He was lying there, ruining our lives the way he was so good at, and I unwillingly let go, all my negative emotions toward him pouring out of my mouth before I could stop them. As my opening line of "what the fuck?!" tumbled from my soul to my lips, followed by more shocking and probably hurtful profanity-laden sentences, Bern looked at me…and he smiled. The look on his face was pure admiration.

That smile of his could light up any room and any heart. Here was my 20 year old intimidating as hell brother that I had come to hate because of his anger, smiling at me like the little boy he used to be; the one who taught me to jump off the roof of the barn, to pole vault between hay bales, to climb trees and tie knots and skateboard, the one who had always been my idol; the boy he was before the world and his sorrows had drowned him.

I had been dormant and tolerant for years; the responsible, independent, sober baby sister; the one who worked multiple days per week cleaning houses since elementary school, the one who did the dishes and vacuumed the house and looked after the animals and was always pleasant, and now I was unleashing my fury on him.

I think he was proud of me in that moment; proud of my strength and my willingness to finally fight; to finally admit that I was fucking pissed off. Deep down, in the recesses of my soul, I've always been grateful that he wasn't around to see how I completely lost control of my life and became just as far gone on drugs as he was before he died.

I understand now that it was something no one who loves me should ever have had to witness.

***

It's hard to remember the exact sequence of events; everything that happened is jumbled together and stored inside the part of my mind that's reserved for terrible memories. It's a time that's incredibly painful to visit, but it's also a time that made me who I am and revealed to me the vast reserve of inner strength I possess.

After the news of my brother's murder broke in December of 1997, the days, weeks and months passed with rumors swarming the school halls; I never quite got used to the whispers, the stares, and the instant silence when I walked into a room.

Not only did I feel alone, I realized that I was alone. My sister was living in Colorado, and my parents were living in a hell that no parent should ever have to experience. My friends didn't know how to react to or handle what had just happened to my brother. We were just kids; we were in the throes of trying to figure out who we were as people and this bomb that had just been dropped onto our world was more than we knew what to do with. The entire school it seemed, people I had known since kindergarten, seemed suddenly afraid of me. Very few of them said anything to me about my brother. It seemed as if the community I had been raised within was already trying to forget what had just happened.

The sister of the man who had murdered Bern was one year ahead of me in school. We had been friends from a distance our whole lives, running with the same crowd sometimes, but never really interacting with one another to a depth that mattered. I found her in the school commons a few days after the first article in the local newspaper; the article that named both our families and gave the details of what our brothers had done. Even though her brother pulled the trigger, my brother was not an innocent saint. They were both doing meth, and the mistakes and poor choices that both of them made had led their younger sisters to that place in the school commons, while the entire school looked on with bated breath.

I walked up to her as a hush fell over the commons. I knew they were waiting to see blood. As I closed the distance between us, she put her hands up over her face and begged me not to hurt her. How could anyone ever be that afraid of me?

I wrapped my fingers around her wrists, pulled her hands away from her face, and put my arms around her. She clung to me and sobbed while telling me how sorry she was. I realized that she had lost her brother, too, and I wondered if it was worse to be the sister of the victim, or the sister of a monster.

The horrid newspaper articles continued. Every paper in the state was featuring the story on the front page and continued publishing it for what seemed years to come.

I drifted from the group of girls that had been my best friends since elementary school. I drifted, and they pushed. That first Christmas, when Bern had been buried for only a couple of weeks, my friends wrapped my Christmas gift, a history book about Salem, Massachusetts that I had been wanting, in newspaper. They wrapped it so that Bern's obituary was right on the top of the gift.

They laughed when I noticed, and I laughed, too, though my heart was breaking quietly, not wanting them to feel uncomfortable. I cried later, when I was alone.

I had long ago developed the habit of ensuring that everyone else around me is content, comfortable, and happy, while I solo-slay dragons and demons in the privacy of my own head and heart. I was never fully aware of it, though, until 2014 when I was crewing aboard the Liseron in Alaska and one of the deckhands commented on my "need to be needed". His words, not meant to be harsh, nor necessarily complimentary, just simply an observation on his part, stopped me in my tracks. He barely knew me, but he was dead on. I've spent my life ensuring that everyone else is happy – boyfriends, friends, employers – while I bury everything about me deep down inside.

We buried my brother on December 13, 1997, in our private cemetery on the J Diamond L Ranch.

Watching my mom stoically deal with the murder of her oldest child was a heartbreaking tragedy that sometimes felt more tragic to me than my brother's death.

As his body laid before us in the coffin a woodworker friend had generously made, my mom gently laid her hand on her son, a body bag separating her palm from his remains. She was so strong. I still don't know how she survived it; how any of us survived it.

Murder is something that happens in movies, not to your classmate, your friend, your brother. People kept their distance, and I was battling too much shock to know how to even attempt to talk about it with anyone.

Bern's funeral was the first time I had openly cried. I remember burying my grandpa, when I was 13, and feeling humiliated and shamed that one single tear had escaped and was rolling down my cheek. I also remember my aunt noticing and telling me that crying didn't mean I was weak.

I've had a lifelong struggle with my feelings towards crying, yet at Bern's funeral, it was all too much. Everyone around me was sobbing, and the feeling of emptiness that was inside me filled itself with all the tears I had been too afraid to shed until it overflowed.

We had each brought something to put inside Bern's coffin. I searched for weeks to find the perfect thing but was still empty-handed only days before the funeral. But I knew that I would know it when I saw it, whatever it turned out to be.

The day before his funeral, I walked around Ashland, Oregon with friends. Wandering into the infamous hippy store, Rare Earth, I was pulled toward the most perfect gift for my brother.

Jerry Garcia had died two years earlier, in 1995, and Bern had mourned, along with Dead Heads the world over. He had adored the Grateful Dead, and there, sitting on the shelf in Rare Earth, was a sticker that depicted, colorful Grateful Dead style, Jerry Garcia walking down a golden path toward a bright light. On either side of him, Dead Bears held his hands, and written across the top was 'Fare thee well'.

To this day, I wish desperately that I had bought two of those stickers – one for Bern, and one for me, to remind me of Bern.

As I placed his sticker inside his coffin, setting it gently on top of the body bag, all my shame about public crying vanished, and I cried for my brother like I never had before, and never have since, cried for any person.

As I cut through the library one day between classes, the librarian called me to her desk and handed me an envelope with my name on it. Though I didn't know what it was, I thanked her and walked away. I stood in the hall and opened the envelope. It was a photocopy of the newspaper article about Bern's death with a note saying that she thought I might want it, to keep for myself.

My mom had been clipping all the articles to put into a binder. I never remember her showing me any of them, though I don't remember her trying to keep them from me either. The librarian had just offered me the gift of healing that no one else had – she acknowledged Bern's death, and she acknowledged that I was hurting, too, not just my parents.

I went back to the library every day after that to collect my envelope from the librarian. One of the possessions I now treasure the most is my book of newspaper articles. It's always with me, no matter where I go, and only one person has ever seen it.

***

The trial took place during my senior year of high school. I had to take notes to my teachers explaining why I would be missing a week of school. None of them required that I make up the work or do homework. None of them knew what to say or how to handle it.

I remember feeling nothing as I sat on that hard bench in the Jackson County courtroom and stared at the back of the head of the guy that killed my brother; a guy we had all grown up with. I remember feeling unnerved that I felt nothing. The numbness of shock was so severe. I was already thin, but I lost 20 pounds that week; starving myself due to the horrific images of death breeding inside my overactive teenaged mind.

I spent nearly a year sleeping on the floor at the foot of my parents' bed after Bern died. I'm not super proud of that fact, but shit, my brother had just been murdered.

When I turned 17, I decided that it was time to sleep in my own room, directly across the hall from my parent's room. We both left our doors open. In the middle of the night, with tears and sweat soaking my body, I crept into my parent's room and found my sleeping bag still made up on the floor, waiting for me.

The trial resulted in Cameron Perry being sentenced to 25 years in the Oregon State Penitentiary. No parole and lifetime probation. The other two men who were involved walked away with time-served (one year in county jail).

Bern had been murdered on his 21st birthday, and his killer was sentenced on my 19th birthday.

After Bern's death, my life became a hellish nightmare that I will cherish forever. I became heavily involved in drugs and became so mentally and emotionally crippled that I was a hollow shell of the person I used to be.

My days were filled with medications I couldn't pronounce, therapists I wouldn't talk to, and debilitating sleeping pills that provided no relief from the realistic and horrifying images that haunted me at night. I was numb, and so desperately wanted to feel alive, to feel something, to feel anything. Most days, I couldn't make it to nightfall without feeling the bite of a blade on my skin.

With my self-worth dashed and my mind reeling with confusion, I was taken to a place between life and the brink of death. I so desperately wanted to die, but I was terrified of actually dying. Feeling as if I were out of options, I turned to drugs.

I forced my mind, and therefore my body, to challenge death; a challenge meant to make me feel something.

It began with small things, such as not wearing my seatbelt, to bigger things, such as taking any pill that was handed to me at a party without asking what it was, to huge things, such as getting behind the wheel of my car when I couldn't even remember what I had done five minutes prior, or what drugs I had taken that day.

I remember crawling into the driver seat one night while saying aloud to my friends "am I really the one driving? This just doesn't seem safe". Yet I was laughing while I shoved down the sensible part of me that knew I was making the wrong decision.

That night resulted in many horrors, including watching my friend get beaten by her drunken boyfriend, me being beaten for trying to help her, a sobbing and terrified phone call to my boyfriend begging him to come help us, a desperate phone call to 911, jumping from my parked car moments before a head-on collision with a truck doing nearly 100 miles per hour, the arrest of a wild and uncontrollable friend, and finally, holding my friend, both of us bruised, bloodied, and broken while she had a miscarriage on the floor of a hotel bathroom.

This was my life. I knew I was sinking fast into the pits of hell, and I knew I needed help. Yet I didn't know how to ask for help. I was still that prideful girl who never asked for what she needed. I was also deeply ashamed to voice aloud to anyone the reality of how far I had allowed myself to fall. I know now that strength can also be a weakness.

I felt so deeply that I had been wronged by life; that this was all there was for me because my veins held Miller blood. People judged me based on their knowledge of my brother's murder, and I felt that my family was embarrassed by who my biological father was. I never believed that I could amount to anything great. Yet deep down, I knew that my brother would be horrified and ashamed of the person I had become since his death.

I was acting as if I were the victim instead of him. The anger, the pain, the confusion, and the hollow emptiness were consuming me, and the vicious cycle of getting high to avoid the pain had become a routine necessity. I could no longer handle reality. I could no longer handle the fact that my brother, the man I adored and worshiped, the man who was so strong, had been savagely ripped from this life. The thought of my big, tough brother being put in such a state of weakness terrified me and made me realize that no one is invincible, even if you're strong, and even if you have a gun in the back of your pants.

As is common with life, time moves on, with or without you. The days, weeks, months and years ticked by while I spent them in a drug-induced haze, oblivious to the pain I was causing those around me. I was so cruel to my parents. My own pain blinded me and made me selfish. Taking advantage of the fact that my parents were pre-occupied with legal details, I would call my mom from school and tell her that I just couldn't handle school that day and ask if she would excuse me. She always did. It started out innocently, with my friends and I going to Dutch Brothers Coffee and simply talking while we drank vast amounts of caffeine. But we never talked about Bern. We never talked about his death.

After a few weeks, I stopped calling my mom asking for permission to leave school and just started ditching. But this time it was to hang out with my brother's friends. My brother's older, cooler, drug-using friends. I lied to my mom at first about who I was hanging out with, but I stopped giving a shit about anything, especially her opinion, so I would ditch school and spend my days with the 'bad kids'.

At first, I wasn't using drugs with them because they didn't offer any to me. It was almost like they were afraid that Bern would walk through the door at any minute and bust them for being bad influences on me. His death was still so surreal.

Time faded quickly, and they started offering me drugs. I was so young; so naïve and in so much pain. They would make comments about how much like my brother I was while they were passing me the bottle, or the joint, or the pipe. All I had ever wanted was for my brother to think I was cool, and suddenly here I was hanging with his crowd, one of the cool bad kids. But he wasn't there. He wasn't there to stop me, so I tumbled into that dark, unforgiving world that had once been his, with no one to catch my fall.

I felt like an imposter. I went along with it all and did all the drugs and laughed while we ruined our lives, but I always knew I was fucking up. There were times when I would become so suddenly overcome with the knowledge of the mistakes I was making that it would nearly choke me. So many times, I simply got up off the couch and walked out into the dark night alone while they continued to party. I can't even count how many times I walked multiple miles home in the dark, completely fucked up on drugs and alcohol, alone on the dark streets of Wimer, Oregon.

A night that haunts my memory is Valentine's Day of 1998. I found myself again at a party, doing things I shouldn't have been doing. I quickly discovered that being the little sister of someone who had recently been murdered made me a pseudo-celebrity. People felt sorry for me, and they weren't quite sure what to say to me, so they handed me copious amounts of drugs and mumbled their apologies for my loss. Being murdered had drastically upped my brother's cool factor, which made me cool simply because I shared DNA with someone who had been shot in the face multiple times. Everyone knew who I was, and everyone wanted to give me drugs as a ceremonious contribution to my brother's memory. So, I took their drugs. I let them slip their wares into my palm, free of charge, of course, and I ingested them, not asking until later, when I was completely gone from reality, what it was I had taken.

That terrible Valentine's party was four months after Bern had died, but only two months since his body had been found. As I stood around the bonfire, watching and sadistically laughing (thanks to the drugs) as a good friend nearly set himself ablaze in his fucked-up stupor, I realized that I didn't feel the way I was supposed to feel; I wasn't supposed to feel anything, yet as I stood mesmerized by the flames, I felt it all. Every gunshot. Every tear he cried. Every handful of dirt he clutched between his fingers while he tried to crawl away.

Panicking, I searched out a trusted friend and confided that I wasn't feeling right. He laughed and told me that the weed I had been smoking incessantly all night had been laced with PCP. The combination of drugs I had taken that night was staggering. How was I still alive?

In my disoriented state, all I wanted was to be home, away from the visions of my brother's murder, safe in my bed, where my parents thought I was.

And so, I walked away from the party, my back growing cold as my distance from the fire increased. I walked, and I walked. I was enshrouded by the pitch black of night, and I cried as I walked and begged my brother to help me. I begged him to let me die, to take me to wherever he was, because I simply had no strength left within me to continue living this miserable and painful life.

I sank to my knees on the abandoned street and screamed out to him, my face to the sky, the stars blurring through my tears and my breath clouding the bitter February air. Then, I started to run; I ran with everything I had, my chest burning and my head spinning.

When I finally reached my bedroom window, I climbed inside and sat on the floor, rocking back and forth, holding myself tightly and crying as I came down off PCP, and my pleas to my dead brother changed – from asking for death, to asking for help getting clean. I asked him to help me not end up like him.

I made it through that horrific night by listening to music. That feeling of swimming across my bedroom floor while lying on my back in the dark, headphones in, music turned up. It was a feeling of escape. It was the feeling of letting the music take me to a different place, a better place; a place where I was finally safe.

That's how I survived my brother's death, with the medicating tunes of Floater, a Portland, Oregon band that I partially credit with saving my life. Their music was my soul-healing escape.

I would lay in the dark for hours, letting the rhythm and that God-like voice stitch together the pieces of my shattered existence.

My brother introduced me to Floater's music before he died; the band was a favorite among our crowd of degenerates. After his death, we dubbed one of their songs in his honor and played it loud, all of us lying on the floor, bodies scattered like ashes in the darkness while we drifted together on our high.

The music saved me; it was one of the only things that saved me. I couldn't let myself die, because I couldn't imagine not being surrounded by the life-changing music of Floater, and I couldn't imagine putting my mother through losing another child.

I would drift and tangle myself up in their lyrics; words that were so deep and rich and laced with such meaning that it was painfully and beautifully profound.

As ridiculous as it sounds to some, I chose to live because of that band. I lived for them, and anyone who is a true music lover will understand the power of that.

Years later, when I was clean and sober, I began working for Floater booking shows, doing promotion, and working the merchandise table at shows. Knowing them as people and loving their music on such a deep level made me (and still makes me) want to not only survive, but truly thrive. Their music, and their friendship, brought me back from the place where I had spent so long balancing on the cliff of oblivion.

A few days after the Valentine's party, I sat on a damp log in the forest with Mike, the friend who was with my brother the last time I saw him, while the brilliant winter sunshine made us both squint and look down at our feet. As far gone as Mike was on drugs, he seemed to sense that I was even farther gone.

After a deep drag off his cigarette, Mike cleared his throat. "You know, Bern told me once that he would give his life if it meant keeping you off drugs."

I stared at my black combat boots while my throat burned with tears that threatened to claw their way out. The tears had their way. As the salty emotion rolled down my cheeks I lit another cigarette and blinked behind my sunglasses. Unable to utter any words that would do justice to what Mike had just told me, I sat nodding my head up and down while the crunchy leaves at my feet blurred through my tears.

To this day, I don't know if my brother actually said that, or if Mike saw that I was fading fast and needed saving. Either way, it was what I needed to change my life.

I honestly don't remember when I finally stopped using drugs; I don't have one last hurrah to recall like most addicts; I don't have a date on the calendar where I give thanks every year it passes, and I'm still sober. All I have is the knowledge that one day I was an alcoholic and drug addict, and the next day, I wasn't. And that's enough for me. I had finally realized the power I held within myself; I saw that I was strong, that I had incredible will-power, and that I wanted to live.

So, I chose life. And I chose to live a happy life. I was exhausted from feeling sorry for myself; I was exhausted from seeing the people I loved dread spending time with me. I had become a miserable, bitter person who dwelled upon the negative in my life, completely blind to the vast amounts of positive, because really, there's always positive - you just have to want to see it.

It was near-instantaneous, this change of mine, and when I look back to the person I used to be, that lost and desperate girl, it oftentimes takes me a moment to realize that it was me - that we are one and the same, yet so changed between then and now.

I had a friend say to me once that when he first met me he had the impression that I was a woman who had never experienced any hardships in life because of the confidence and happiness I portray to the world. He knows now, after many deep conversations, that my confidence and my happiness are things I've worked hard for; things I haven't always possessed. The person I became after my brother's death is someone that no one who knows me now would ever recognize; someone who no one would ever believe I could have been. That dark and horridly sad person is someone I hold hidden deep inside me, and only a few have ever heard the stories associated with her. I had decided to live the best life I possibly could despite my past, and because of my past.

***

My parents have always been my biggest fans, and a great part of being able to change was because of them. And by parents, I mean my mom and step-dad. They have always supported my unconventional lifestyle; they've never asked me, like so many others, when I'm going to settle down and find myself a man and give them grandkids. They know that I'm living life exactly the way I want to, and I love them to the depths of my soul for simply wanting me to be happy.

I will never forget the exact moment I realized that my step-dad, Bruce, was the father I was always meant to have. My biological father, Paul, still had visitation, and he was meant to pick us up one night and take us to the movies. I don't remember how old I was, but it was after the Colorado incident.

My brother and sister didn't want to go, but I put on my best dress and could hardly contain my excitement about seeing my daddy. My mom and step-dad weren't married yet, and I was struggling with potentially having a new father figure.

When Paul was hours late, my brother and sister went to bed. When he was still more hours late, my mom went to bed. Yet there I sat on the couch in the living room, watching out the picture window for headlights on the driveway until late into the night. And there sat Bruce right next to me. He sat there with me all night waiting for my father. Neither of us talked; he simply held my hand, watching my little girl heart be broken by a man for the very first time.

I awoke the next morning in my bed, my dress rumpled around my legs and my cheeks stained with dried tears. Bruce had carried me to bed after I had fallen asleep waiting for Paul. I was too young to realize the depth of Bruce's love for me back then, but that was the moment I accepted him as my dad and stopped holding out hope that my father would come back to me.

I now realize how intensely fortunate I am to have been given a step-dad who has always loved me like his own. He is the greatest man on this earth; kind, humble, and loving, and I am so thankful for his presence in my life that sometimes it is a physical hurt.

My mother – now she is something else. In high school English class, we were given an assignment to write about our hero. It could be anyone, and for any reason. Most students wrote about historical figures. I wrote about my mom, because she is the strongest woman I have ever known. She has a heart the size of Alaska and a capacity for forgiveness that is staggering.

Of course, as is common with daughters and mothers, I didn't always appreciate her best qualities. In fact, I remember being horrified by them when she forgave one the men who was involved in my brother's murder.

It was years after Bern's death when Chris threw himself on the mercy of my family and begged for forgiveness. My mother gave it to him. I did not.

Chris began coming to family dinners and stopping by the house randomly for visits. With no family of his own, he was looking not only to be forgiven, but to belong. I would leave the house when Chris would come over, and I would make a dramatic, door-slamming exit to let Chris, and everyone else know that I absolutely did not accept this new member of our family. Basically, I was a hurtful bitch to Chris, something that makes me cringe with shame now.

It took me years to be okay with his presence. He would often tell my mom to relay messages to me; saying that he was willing to sit down with me and answer any questions I had about the day Bern died, something he had done for my mom and sister. He was offering the best form of closure that he was able to provide.

The day came when I hit a wall with my anger; I was exhausted from being pissed off that my brother had died. One day, when my parents weren't home, I slipped the binder of printed confessions from the bookshelf where my mother kept it. It was literally that – printed transcripts from when the men involved in my brother's murder had been questioned by the police at the local fire station.

I flipped to Chris's section and began to read. It's bizarre to read a transcript and attempt to picture the scene in your mind. The italic statements of *"suspect begins to cry"* and *"suspect vomits"* create images that are very far removed while you're sitting in the sunshine reading about murder.

Yet it became clear that Chris was a 19-year-old boy who was a classic example of wrong-place, wrong-time. I had always refused to believe that he didn't know Cameron was going to kill my brother. I had always vehemently believed that he was just as guilty as the others. But as my anger faded with time, my heart softened and became open enough to receive the truth.

I called Chris and told him that I was ready to face him; I was ready to talk to him about the day my brother died.

We met at Olive Garden in Medford, Oregon for dinner. He parked next to me in the lot and got into the passenger seat of my car to say hello out of the rain. We never opened the doors again until hours later. We sat there in the parking lot all night talking and remembering Bern. Olive Garden closed, and still we sat in the car, and I forgave him.

It became so very clear to me that night in the Olive Garden parking lot just how much Chris had suffered when Bern died, and how he continued to suffer. Sure, my brother died and that had affected my entire life and will never stop affecting me. But Chris was there; he witnessed something too shocking for most people to comprehend. He had nightmares, too, just as I did, but his were because he had watched someone die.

I rarely tell people that I've forgiven one of the men who was involved in my brother's murder. And not only did I forgive him, I accepted him, and he now belongs. He will forever be a part of my family. He will forever be a brother to me.

I rarely tell people because their reaction is usually shock and anger. They don't understand how my family could forgive when something so precious was ripped away from us, but no one could ever possibly know what they would do if they watched their best friend and roommate kill another friend. People make mistakes; often tragic mistakes. Chris had the courage to ask for forgiveness. My family had the courage to give it to him. It takes so much effort to stay angry, yet you only need to muster the energy once to forgive.

Chapter Six

"I know what you are, and it's scaring me to death" Floater

I was surprised by how much I adored Friday Harbor, a relatively small island of about 8,000 year-round residents. I immediately made wonderful friends and fell easily into island life.

As has always been common for me, boredom was dispelled by working multiple jobs. My first summer on the island I had four jobs. I worked the early morning shift at a café, the afternoon shift in an office making reservations for a whale watch boat (Friday Harbor's main tourist attraction is the Southern Resident Killer Whales), and I worked the evening shift aboard another whale watch boat. Six days per week I worked three jobs in one day. Every Friday I spent all day working aboard an inflatable boat operated by a non-profit called Soundwatch. We spent our time wherever the whales were, enforcing the federal whale watch regulations. Essentially, we were the whale police; ensuring the whale watch boats abided by the rules.

On the next island over, a one mile paddle across San Juan Channel in a kayak, yet an hour ride aboard the Washington State interislander ferry, was Shaw Island. And on Shaw lived my first legit boyfriend since leaving my husband five years prior. This guy was sexy. Man bun, firefighter, tiny home builder, world traveler with a washboard stomach. Oh, how looks can deceive. By the end of our short relationship, he had become so ugly to me that my stomach turned just by making eye contact with him.

Only a few weeks in I began to realize that he was a possessive stage five clinger with severe mommy issues, which he thoroughly projected onto me. Yet on the surface he was kind and giving and attentive and my friends scoffed when I voiced my unhappiness with him. He gave me gifts all the time (an act that triggered the memories of my unhappy marriage). His gift-giving, however, was a way for him to keep score. He once listed off to me all the gifts he had given me and then said, "and all you've given me is a hummingbird feeder".

Number one, that hummingbird feeder was thoughtful, asshole. And number two, as my buddy Alex and I say — "but also, fuck you."

I spent my first summer in Friday Harbor feeling as if I were insane; wondering what the hell was wrong with me that I wasn't happy with this (supposedly) amazing guy that (supposedly) loved me. I resented the fact that he wanted (needed!) to talk to me on the phone every single night for hours on end. I was bitter about the fact that when I wouldn't respond to his text messages immediately (did I mention my four jobs…) he would then become pouty and ask me if we were "okay". And I desperately dreaded the one night per week that he would take the ferry from Shaw to Friday Harbor to spend the night with me.

He felt like an obligation, and I felt like a bitch for feeling like he was an obligation. I was distant and guarded and he called me on it all the time. I was constantly stressed out, on edge, and jumpy. Yet it had been so long since I'd had a relationship that I thought maybe this was normal. Relationships are hard work, right? Well, they definitely are when you're in one with a fucking psycho.

Near the end of summer, I finally realized that this dude was manipulating me and attempting to turn me into something I was not. He would politely and sweetly tell me that I shouldn't be friends with overweight people because it showed a lack of self-respect on my part for being friends with someone who was "unhealthy". He would tearfully tell me that he wasn't comfortable with me being friends with the dreadlocked kayak guide because he knew that other men found me attractive.

This guy's subtle mind-control via affection and concern was off the charts. He made me feel like a bitch for not wanting to tell him all the dirty details about my past and made me feel like even more of a bitch for not crying every time I saw him (he cried every time he saw me, and it was beyond embarrassing).

I had winter plans to head to Florida and go to Sea School to obtain my Captain's license. This had been the plan since before I met Shaw Boy. In early September, after five months of dating, he told me that he didn't want me to get my Captain's license because it would open doors for me that might take me away from him. I told him to fuck off. And that's how I broke up with him. With a text message literally telling him to fuck off. Not my most diplomatic move, but it felt damn good.

In hindsight, I'll admit that I definitely was guarded and distant with him, and rightfully so. My mind didn't understand at the time why I was being that way, but the very core of me knew that he was not a person who deserved to truly know the inner me.

***

My fear of men had been instilled in me at a very young age. I grew up in a troubled home, dealing with an abusive alcoholic father. I knew the way I saw my father treat my mother was wrong, and I promised myself that I would never find myself in a similar situation. Yet I did.

My first marriage, at the age of 22, was turbulent, violent, and filled with anger. It lasted a year and a half and ended when another woman turned up pregnant with my husband's child. But that pregnancy was the greatest thing to happen to me at that point in time; it saved my life, it saved my future. I left, and then married my second husband several years later.

My second marriage, for all its greatness, was filled with flaws of its own (what marriage isn't?), and even though it was me who chose to leave, it broke my heart none-the-less. I've had three boyfriends since my divorce in 2011, two of which I'm still unclear as to if we were actually in a labeled relationship, and the longest of which lasted only six months and ended tragically, leaving the glaring summer sun glinting upon the shards of my shattered heart.

I've always felt that perhaps, due to that fear of men, I subconsciously sabotage my relationships, and in most of them, I've been the one to do the leaving. At the first hint of rejection, I run. I've always been that way. I leave first, so they don't have the chance to. I'm sure my biological father's choice to leave when I was a child has something to do with that. How could it not?

The few times my second ex-husband talked about his father's death, I remember thinking 'at least he didn't *choose* to leave you', and then thinking to myself what a bitch I was for allowing that thought to enter my mind. The absence of a father is felt deeply, no matter how the leaving occurred.

But this trouble with men has been a reoccurring theme in my life. I want to be loved, I long to be loved, but I'm not quite sure how to be loved. I expect heartbreak, so I keep my distance, and the few times I have let my walls down just a little, I've been hurt. I expect it, therefore perhaps I manifest it. And yet somehow, I'm always surprised.

I had a friend reach out to me recently about a heartbreak he had experienced. He was asking advice on how to deal with it; wondering how I deal with it since it seems to happen to me often (gee, thanks...), and he wondered how I stay consistently single without being lonely. My question is how do others find partners? I never can seem to. It's a skill I am apparently lacking.

My friend Mere says that she and I must have missed that day in school when they took all the girls aside and taught them how to find boyfriends. I think she's probably right. I don't mind being alone, but I want someone to share my life with. However, after being alone for so long, I have these ideals about the man I would allow into my life, and I'm not willing to compromise; to have the wrong boyfriend simply for the sake of having a boyfriend. I'm still trying to figure out if that's strength, or a stubborn downfall.

I've realized in the past few years of my life that the independence I've clung to so fiercely is actually a hindrance in my life, and while I'm not suggesting that I'm about to part with that independence, I've had my eyes opened to the fact that I can let go a little bit; I can open up and trust and learn to rely on the people in my life who care about me when I need help, whether those people be friends or a man. I've learned to understand that I'm not actually on my own and alone in this world, like I've always told myself I am. This realization, my epiphany, came from meeting my biological father in late 2015 for the first time since I was six years old.

It had been nearly 30 years since my father and I had gazed upon one another. I was a child the last time he saw me. He was in handcuffs the last time I saw him.

We met at a Subway restaurant in Nevada, Missouri. I was on my solo cross-country road trip, destined for Florida where I would spend the next two months going to school to get my captain's license. I was sick with nerves, and confessed to my cousin via text message that I might puke. She reminded me to think of how nervous he must be. He had everything to be sorry for; everything to be ashamed of. He probably hadn't changed too terribly much, physically, in those nearly 30 years but I, however, had become a woman. I was no longer that little girl he remembered.

And she was right – he looked, for the most part, exactly as I had remembered him. When I pulled up next to his van and got out of my Jeep, his first words to me were "who the hell are you?!". I can only imagine that it was far more bizarre for him to see me, grown and independent, than it was for me to see him.

After lunch, accompanied by his absolutely lovely wife, we went back to their house, a ranch-style home on roughly 80 acres in the middle of gorgeous Missouri fields and forest. My dad took me for a ride around the property on his Polaris ATV and we talked of our mutual passion for seafaring and world travel. This, I realized, was where my difference came from; he was why I was different from the rest of the family I had known all my life. I finally had the explanation I had always sought, and it created within me a feeling of peace that I had never before known. Yet it also created a feeling of unease, knowing that what everyone back home thought of me was actually true – I was so much, too much, like my father. Damn that Miller blood.

After dinner, I sat on the porch swing with my dad's wife. A storm was brewing, and lighting sparked within dark orange clouds that hovered over the back field. As we rocked back on forth in unison and talked, I watched my father walking away across the field, his faithful dog, Charlie, by his side, off on their nightly perimeter check of the fence line. He was wearing the same type of shirt I remember from my childhood – a plain white Hanes t-shirt; the same type of shirt he was wearing the last time I saw him when I was a child in Colorado.

I kept my gaze fixed on him as he grew smaller with distance, eventually only seeing a flash of white between trees as he disappeared into the darkening forest. It was surreal, watching him, being at his house, fat raindrops clinking slowly upon the tin roof of his porch. I was at my dad's house. After nearly 30 years, I had finally met my father. The one hope of my entire life, and I had just achieved it.

I screamed out loud as I drove away that night, after declining their invitation to stay. It was too soon for a slumber party. I wanted, needed, to be alone and process the day I had just had. A day with my dad. As I drove through the building storm, lightening flashing all around my car, I rolled down all the windows, allowing the rain to cleanse my face, and at the top of my lungs, I shouted my thanks to the wind and to whichever deity would listen: God, the Great Spirit, Allah, Buddha, my brother. I thanked them all while I joyfully laughed in the face of Mother Nature's fury.

***

After all the years of being on my own, yet somehow seeming to always find myself in the company of drunken assholes, I had finally given up on men and resigned myself to the single-girl life of unwanted advances from the dudes you have no interest in, no advances from the ones you are interested in, and people always (always) asking why you're single because you're so nice/pretty/funny/smart, etc.

But as is common with fairytales (if you hadn't noticed, this isn't one...), the moment I broke up with hope, was the moment I found love again, or so I had thought.

He was presented to me in the form of a charming redhead, complete with the most adorable dimples and a laugh that came easily, at least in the beginning. I gave into him and the love that felt so natural with a reckless abandon like I never had before with any of the others. I allowed all my walls to crumble; I turned my back on my notion that all men were evil and would eventually break my heart. This was it. He was it. I had finally found this mythical 'one' that women are forever referring to, albeit usually with tears in their eyes.

We spent our days on our island in the sea, commuting via ferry, living aboard the sailboat with my cat, watching the setting sun cast diamonds across the ocean and listening to harbor seals breathe while we gazed up toward my favorite constellation, Orion.

Eventually, we moved together to Bellingham. Six months later, however, I inevitably found myself aboard the Washington State Ferry, headed back out to Friday Harbor, San Juan Island, the romantic little place off the coast of Seattle where our love had blossomed, to return his grandmother's ring to his mother. I was headed out alone, to the island where he and I met; where we were co-workers first, then friends, then stupidly in love with one another. I looked out upon Puget Sound, feeling the comforting rumble of the ferry, and wondered... how the fuck did I get here?? Mid-thirties, broke (financially), broken (emotionally), and with absolutely no clue what to do next.

It came as a shock, him abandoning me the way he did, like he said he never would. Where had our happiness gone? Where had his integrity gone? I'm sure they're floating in the dregs of his beer bottle, along with a few cigarette butts, left to bloat in the remains of the liquid that destroyed us.

Those islands, where I was so happy, held no comfort for me any longer. The Pacific Northwest, where I was born and raised, where I always go back to no matter how long I've been away, had uncurled its tree-lined fingers from my heart and I saw now its true form – dreary, grey, and damp. The Salish Sea had spat out my soul, once held in its depths, and I felt numb to its salt-soaked magic.

At one point or another, we've all felt that terrible feeling of being so utterly lost and confused and too numb to make any decisions. The heaviness deep in your chest, the sick feeling in your stomach where you're not sure if you're starving because you've been too heart-sick to eat in days, or if you're going to vomit because you're, well...heart-sick, and that awful tightness in your throat from trying so damn hard not to cry.

Pathetically, I kept telling myself, "but he was supposed to be different". Well, he wasn't. Whoever said it's better to have loved and lost, then to never have loved at all...was full of shit. I wish I could throat-punch that person. What's the point of loving if the other person is going to stomp all over your exposed heart and everything the two of you had built?

The months that followed that breakup, they were torturous. I thought I had hit rock bottom before, so many times throughout my life, yet now, with my insides figuratively splattered across the canyon floor, I realized that *this* was actually rock bottom. This was deeper than rock bottom, because all the fight to survive had gone out of me, and I found myself living in my Jeep, illegally residing in a parking garage on the other side of the country from anything and everyone I knew.

I'm a runner (and I don't mean the marathon type), and I was so concerned with running as far and as fast from this last disappointment of a man that I ended up in Salem, Massachusetts. You might think "ooohhh, how brave, how unconventional," to be so free and not paying rent, but let me assure you that bravery was not involved in this. Unconventional, maybe. Bravery, hell no. This was out of desperation and a sheer fight-or-flight adrenaline. Living in the parking garage was due to the simple fact that I had nowhere else to live. My heart was destroyed, and I was living in a parking garage. It sounds tragic, and at the time, it was. Again, how the fuck did I get here?

I kept reminding myself that there was a lesson here somewhere. Somewhere, hidden beneath the piles of belongings in the back of the Jeep, in which I could never find what I was looking for, there was a lesson. Maybe it was under the mound of dirty clothes collecting behind the driver seat. I hadn't checked there yet.

I realize now that for all my 'running', I was never actually running *from*...I was running *to* – to a place where I had friends, where I had a place to crash and the promise of companionship and understanding. To the next adventure. This time, I was definitely running *from*. I was running from him. I was so desperate to put as much distance between us that I simply got in my car and drove. No plan, really, just driving...all the way to the other side of the country because it was the farthest away from him I could get without actually leaving the country (though I did look into leaving the country as well). I had never been so devastated, confused, and hurt in my life. I had never been so disappointed in, and disgusted by someone in all my life.

With a nation separating us, I still didn't understand how he could choose his love of alcohol over his love for me, except to rationally accept that he never truly loved me at all. So many women reading this will understand that confusion, that earth-shattering blow to the ego. Being slapped in the face with the realization that all of it, everything, was a damn lie. And we still can't help but wonder what we did wrong.

I realize now that I didn't do anything wrong. I did everything right by standing by his side and supporting him emotionally and financially when he had burned every bridge he had ever walked across. Any woman who has ever had the misfortune of loving an alcoholic will forever be reminded of her "failures" and her "inadequacies" every time she stands next to a man who wreaks of alcohol and mint gum.

He and I ended with no warning, really. No warning, except the thousands of red flags I had been ignoring for the past six months, and his increasing alcohol consumption. Moving in together was a giant leap of faith for me; for both of us, I'm sure. I hadn't lived with a boyfriend since my divorce so many years earlier. Reality slapped him in the face and the daily adult responsibilities of not spending every cent on booze were too much for him to absorb. While I waited in line at the food bank, dripping with the sickening feeling of worthlessness, he roamed the town with his buddies, drinking. While his truck sat broken down on the side of the road, I drove him to work every day and eventually went crawling to a friend whom I had already asked so much of for help towing it home. I felt like a single mother with an unappreciative and spoiled child.

But I loved him, and I had so much faith in him, and in us. I would have done anything to make him happy. I didn't want to run anymore. And that is precisely where I went wrong. Concern for his happiness overshadowed my own, and the stress of working three jobs and wondering where he was when he didn't come home for days on end with no word was too much for me.

I borrowed money from friends in order to pay rent, something I've never done before and hope to never have to do again. I stopped eating, out of stress and lack of money, and lost nearly 40 pounds when I was already slender. I cried and cried and survived off coffee and cigarettes and drove myself crazy trying to figure out what was so wrong with me that the boyfriend I lived with would just stop coming home. He had simply vanished. No phone call. No text message. No Facebook message. He was just gone.

The first of August was rapidly approaching, which meant rent was due and I only had my half that I had borrowed. I had no idea what to do. When my messages to him went unanswered, I listed our house on Craigslist for a lease takeover. Still there was no word from him. I found someone to take over our lease and move in on August first. Still, nothing from him. I spent days on end moving all my things out, alone, taking everything to Goodwill, and sending him messages telling him he needed to come move his things as well. Silence.

After a long and exhausting day at work as a kayak instructor, I came home late to an empty house. Completely empty. He had been there while I was at work and moved all his things out. Still, he didn't contact me. I stood in the open doorway of the little house we had shared with so much pain in my heart that it was impossible to even cry. It was impossible to be angry. It was impossible to feel anything at all.

Without ever walking inside the house, I closed the front door and walked back to my car. I sat with the car door open, still wearing my wetsuit and damp shoes from work, sea salt drying on my skin and cigarette smoke billowing around my face in the dark July heat. I turned my eyes up to Orion, the constellation that has guided me since my childhood, and I reverted to the desperation of the years after my brother's death.

***

I had them all lined up; tiny little pill soldiers on a crusade to rid me of my life once and for all. The empty bottle sat on my dashboard and my now-unstoppable tears bled the pink dye off the little warriors I held in my hand, the rest waiting patiently on the dashboard to join them.

I took Benadryl sometimes to sleep, but my intent now was to never wake up. Terror clutched at my heart and my rational brain, but was overshadowed by the emptiness into which I had been cast. There was really no pain at that point, just a dull numbness and overwhelming disbelief.

He and I used to joke about my heartbreaking taxi incident in Australia; being so fully abandoned that now, all these years later, it was almost comical. Yet even though we joked about it, he had promised so many times, with such seeming sincerity, that he would never do that to me; that he would never hurt me so deeply; never walk out on me; never destroy me. But he did all those things.

In that moment in my car in our driveway, engulfed by the night, I couldn't comprehend how a person could make so many empty promises; how they could tell so many lies, masking cowardice with pretty words. I couldn't comprehend how I had been so gullible to it. I had believed every word he told me. I felt like such a fucking fool. I numbly sat there trying to figure out what it was about me that makes no man capable of loving me.

I swallowed half the bottle of Benadryl, choking on my own sobs. I lit yet another cigarette and as I sat quietly, the stars blurred by my tears, I was suddenly overcome with intense fear, so I swallowed the remainder of the bottle. Even though in the moment I wanted that to be the end, I was also keenly aware of my desire to live.

Grabbing my phone, I called my best guy friend and old roommate in Bellingham. Reaching out for emotional help has never been a skill of mine, but desperation will do so many odd things to a person. My crying, pathetic voicemail was heartbreaking...

"I'm sorry to call so late. I know you're at work, but can you please call me when you're off? I'm at the house. He moved all of his stuff out today while I was at work. I'm thinking really stupid thoughts and I don't think I should be alone right now..."

That voicemail went unanswered. The feeling of abandonment deepened.

My eyes had become so heavy from the Benadryl that I couldn't keep them open. My stomach churned and even lighting a cigarette was hindered by the inability to properly use my hands. Fear gripped my chest and my mind. What had I done? Despite it all, I wanted to live. I was not the woman who let a man make her give up; not after all the bullshit I had survived in my life.

Stumbling from my car to the forest across the driveway, I fell to my knees and stuck my fingers down my throat. I choked on my sobs and my vomit while my heart blazed with rage. I stared up at Orion while I lay on my back in the pine needles, next to the thrown-up pills that were nearly my downfall, and I decided for the second time in my life that I would survive, no matter what it took. I decided I would never, ever let a man destroy me again. I am so much better than that. We are all so much better than that. Yet falling apart is vital; it allows us to strip away all the bullshit and rebuild exactly how we desire ourselves to be. Those moments of complete brokenness enable us to truly appreciate the times when we are whole.

The day after that horrid yet profound night when I attempted to take my own life, I got in my car and drove away from Bellingham without telling anyone. 3,000 miles later, I found myself in Salem, Massachusetts, a place where I knew no one, trying to rebuild, to reinvent, to forget. I found myself on the other side of the country from home, destitute, living in the back of my Jeep in a parking garage.

Salem, Mass has called to me since I was a child. I have no idea why. Maybe I saw a photo of it in one of my grandpa's magazines when I was little, or maybe it's because I have been addicted to Halloween my entire life. When the movie Hocus Pocus came out in the early 90's, I dreamed of one day visiting Salem, the "Witch City". When I knew I needed to get as far away from Bellingham as possible, I started driving and ended up in Salem. I will always remember those days of walking cobblestone streets that had existed since the 1600's and feeling the hair on my arms raise when I walked past buildings that were literally saturated in history. Salem was everything I dreamed it would be.

One of my first days in town, I walked into Gulu Gulu Café for a job interview, which I had set up via email during my drive east. As I sat at the counter waiting, a young girl sat down next to me and ordered a waffle. I hadn't eaten in six days. I had no money to eat. I had borrowed yet more money from friends to pay for gas to get me to Salem.

I longingly gazed at her whipped cream-drenched waffle and cleared my throat to cover the hallow sounds of my stomach growling. With no prior words between us, she leaned over and asked if she could buy me a waffle. Initially, I wanted to say no, but my pride had vanished along with my will to live, so I said yes. I can't find words to describe the feeling I experienced due to her amazingly kind gesture to a complete stranger. It was perfectly and exactly the spark of hope I needed during one of the darkest times in my life.

I ended up getting the job at Gulu and made some amazing friends during my time there, one of them being Sophie, the girl who bought me the waffle. I've thanked her so many times since that day, but words could never say what I felt in my heart. Sophie, because of you, I was able to find my footing and begin to climb my way out of rock bottom. I hope that someday I can do the same for someone else.

To look at me, the new girl in town from the Pacific Northwest, no one would have ever guessed that I was homeless. I never told anyone that I was living in the parking garage downtown; that I hid from the security guard while he did his midnight rounds, that I peed in a travel mug in the middle of the night when I couldn't hold it any longer, that I tried unsuccessfully to sleep while sweating off excess pounds in the stifling, muggy heat and then awoke at 4am every morning in order to leave before the first parking garage employee of the day arrived. No one ever knew about the night I cried uncontrollably;

heaving sobs that made my chest burn while I begged God to help me. Me, the unbeliever, crying out to God because I was desperate to survive and felt I had no one left to turn to.

A phone conversation with a friend in Florida had prompted my prayers. As I sat in the driver's seat of the Jeep and talked on the phone with Ronnie, I gazed at the red-lit stained glass of the church across the street from the parking garage; a church that had existed since the early 1600's. Ronnie assured me that God was with me, even though I didn't believe, and he encouraged me to simply talk to Him; to ask Him for help. So I did. I hung up the phone and talked to God. As I talked, I began to cry, and then to sob as I pleaded with an entity that I didn't believe in to help me survive.

The next day, I randomly met a real estate agent in Salem who let me stay for free in an empty apartment. Again, due to the kindness of a stranger, I was given a safe place to sleep at night and access to a bathroom. I spread my air mattress out on the living room floor the first night in the apartment and wept, this time with gratitude. Though I didn't become a converted believer, I was undoubtedly aware that my prayers had in fact been answered. I was safe, I was warm, and I no longer had to pee in a travel mug. And I had a place to sleep to offer my friends from Bellingham who were coming to visit.

***

Have you ever experienced a friendship so deep and profound and genuine that it sometimes breaks your heart? I have. With two people.

I met Jared first, in 2012 when I went into Office Max in Bellingham to print some photos I had taken aboard the Steve Irwin for a gallery showing I was doing. Jared was the guy who printed them. When I came back to pick up the photos, he commented on them and I told him about the showing. He said I should meet his girlfriend, Melissa. A few weeks later we all went to the premier of Blackfish, the documentary my conservation friends had been involved with about orcas in captivity.

All these years later, I can't imagine a time in my life before my friendship with Jared and Melissa. It feels as if they've always been there. Because they always have been there – every time my life falls apart, every time my heart gets broken, every time I go running off and then come crawling home – they are there. I love them so much, and am so grateful for them that it hurts.

They came to visit me in Salem. I was working the counter at Gulu on a busy morning when suddenly Jared was standing before me. The shock of seeing him there, when I was so far from home and feeling so alone, overwhelmed me and I burst into tears. Throwing my arms around his neck, I cried into his shoulder. Poor Jared. I don't think he had any idea what to do.

We spent the next several days roaming the town. I've lived in so many new places that I've become insanely good at directions and learning local customs, to the point where within just a few days I'm able to blend in and navigate like a local. We visited all the famous Hocus Pocus sights, all the old cemeteries, and the Salem Willows, an amusement park on the water. We walked 13 miles in the burning heat and then sat on the rocks at the Willows and ate amazing street food from a filthy looking vendor.

Jared and Melissa are truly my support system; they are consistently there for me through thick and thin, and my words fall short in expressing how much they mean to me.

Salem didn't know just how utterly shattered I was. All they saw was the "strong" and "brave" Pacific Northwest girl who had moved across the country alone to attempt to start over in a place where she knew no one at all. They didn't know, and still they were so kind to me. They took me in, even after everyone had warned me how cold and uninviting East Coasters can be to an outsider. They took me in, and they loved me. The people of Salem will never know how much faith in humanity that provided to my bruised soul.

Chris and Brenda – you'll never know how much that job and the genuine concern touched my numb heart. And Laura, you let me cry. While you fought your own war of life and death, you let me cry. Virginia – you let me stay in your empty apartment when you found out I was living in the parking garage. When you asked where I was living, I considered lying to you because I was ashamed. I'm glad I didn't. And Jamie…my godsend of a friend. How would I have survived Salem without you? All those hours we spent sitting on the porch, smoking cigarettes, talking about music and life. And then you introduced me to Molly. And the two of you became a reason to continue, though I'm not sure you knew it. In a desperately lonely, broken time in my life, so far from home, the two of you provided me with so much kindness. I will never, ever be able to repay you, and I will never, ever be able to convey just how much those porch sessions meant to me. Thank you does not even come close.

You, and your beautiful people, Salem…you all saved my life. Thank you.

Some people collect things. I collect friends. Memories of the friends I've made in the many places I have lived become my souvenirs. Salem was no different.

I departed Salem in a shower of hugs and farewells and pointed my Jeep south, towards Florida, where another set of Souvenir Friends awaited me. I was heading down to do a two-week boat delivery with my very dear captain friend. Once I arrived at his place just north of Tampa, we would fly to Charlottetown, Prince Edward Island and take a 70' luxury Fleming yacht around the outer coast of Nova Scotia, and into Bar Harbor, Maine.

Doug, or the Admiral, as we lovingly call him, taught me virtually everything I know about the maritime industry. He served as the original captain aboard the M/V Liseron for The Boat Company, the vessel I crewed aboard in Alaska and continued to do winter maintenance on in Seattle for many years.

The Boat Company purchased the Liseron in 1989, after her retirement as a mine sweeper for the French military, and refit her into the passenger vessel she is today. Doug oversaw that refit, and my friendship with him is one of the greatest things to come out of my time working for The Boat Company. He is a patient mentor, a caring friend, and a nautical genius.

In late 2015, I spent two months living with Doug in Florida while attending Sea School in St. Petersburg to obtain my 100 ton Master Captain license. Doug tutored me every step of the way, and damn did he crack the whip!

We studied every single day, including weekends, for roughly 12 hours per day. I would sit at his dining room table and pore over charts and text books until my eyes blurred, and my brain literally hurt. I asked question after question, sometimes the same question multiple times, and Doug would patiently answer, with no hint of irritation in his voice. When he could see that I was nearly on the verge of frustrated tears, he would send me outside with a handful of carrots to feed Sugar the pony. And each night he cooked me dinner and we would watch TV and talk late into the muggy Florida nights out on the porch.

When the night of my exams was upon us, I passed all five tests with flying colors and was the only person in my class of 24 to do so. I was also the only girl.

After the tests, I stepped out into the evening with several of my classmates and we stood in the parking lot for a good hour smoking cigarettes and talking. Two of the guys asked me if I would consider tutoring them.

I finally looked at my cell phone, 45 minutes after the allotted test-taking time had ended. Doug had messaged. I clicked open his text on my iphone and saw his words – "Exam ended nearly an hour ago. My stomach is in knots! Fucking call me!"

I laughed and hugged all the boys goodbye, exchanging contact info and promises to keep in touch, and dialed Doug's cell phone as I climbed into my Jeep. I think he nearly sobbed with relief when I told him I passed, but he also told me that he never had a doubt in his mind.

In September of 2016, I found myself heading to Florida from Salem, Mass. Doug and I flew to Prince

Edward Island and walked the dock toward the M/Y Morning Star, the yacht we were to deliver to Bar Harbor. It was late, and we were exhausted from travelling. We tossed our bags aboard and climbed over the starboard side gunwale onto the aft deck. We slipped off our shoes, leaving them on the teak deck and went to the glass sliding doors. They were locked. Doug looked in the usual spot for the keys, but they weren't there. He called the person who had delivered the boat to Charlottetown. He didn't answer. We were locked out.

We spent the next several hours calling hotels and hailing taxis to take us to hotels and having no luck with any of it. It was a holiday weekend in Canada. We finally were able to find two rooms in a run-down hotel on the very far outskirts of town. When we got there, we each mumbled some form of goodnight and dead-bolted our doors. We were burnt out.

The next morning, we were both in better spirits and, with boat key in hand, we headed for the Morning Star.

She was a stunning yacht, and Charlottetown was an equally stunning city. I've been a sappy fan of Anne of Green Gables since I was a child and had always dreamed of visiting Prince Edward Island. Now I was getting paid to be there.

Though Doug and I first met through The Boat Company and had spent time sailing aboard the Liseron together, this was the first time I had crewed with him as captain, and I quickly learned that not only does his reputation proceed him as a captain, but that he deserves every bit (and more) of that reputation. He was as patient as a captain as he was a tutor.

Doug is a unique man in that he is just so chill; so laid-back, so much fun in his ever-present flip-flops (yes, even in Alaska) and Hawaiian shirts and dancing to his favorite band, the Rolling Stones, yet he naturally commands respect. When I first joined the Liseron but had not yet met Doug, I was intrigued by the fact that all the returning crew spoke of this man Doug Cope as if he were some sort of God. They clearly revered him. They had nicknames for him like "Admiral", and even "God". I remember thinking to myself 'who is this guy? He sounds like an arrogant dick head'. And then I met him, and a few days later he and I were dancing to the Rolling Stones while he helped me do dishes in the Liseron galley.

Years later, I found myself dancing to the Rolling Stones on a boat with Doug again. This time in the wheelhouse of the Morning Star as we laughed at Mother Nature while she tossed us around the Bay of Fundy like a rubber ducky. Consistent green water over the gunwale and never-ending spray that made it literally impossible to see was nothing for Doug, and his confidence and competence made it nothing for me either. We cranked up the Stones 'Give me Shelter' and sang and danced and laughed our way through a tropical storm. It was one of the best days of my life.

The next day, with the sea laid down to rest, Doug left me at the helm so he could turn down for a nap. We were far off the eastern coast of Nova Scotia. Sei whales broke the glassy surface as I gazed out onto the mirror of ocean, clouds reflecting on the still sea and the feel of the ships wheel under my palms.

A text came through from my sister, breaking the calmness of the moment. 'I'm sure mom told you about

Wendy. I wanted to say how sorry I am and that I love you'. It's always been shocking to me how one perfect moment can vanish so quickly and be replaced by something so tragic.

I dialed my sister's number but didn't have enough service to make a phone call. I texted back explaining this to her and told her that I had, in fact, not heard about Wendy and could she please explain. As I hit send on my text, Doug walked into the wheelhouse and stood next to me at the helm. I turned to him, found his eyes, and said 'I think my sister just died'.

***

My sister Wendy was diagnosed with breast cancer when she was 42 years old. After her first round of chemo, I drove from Seattle to Vancouver, Washington to visit her. It was the first time we had seen each other in 12 years. We had only begun talking to one another a couple months prior to my visit. Wendy was my half-sister, and though we were raised together, she left home when I was fairly young to move to Salt Lake City. I only saw her two times after she left home. The visit to Vancouver was the third time we had seen each other since I was about seven or eight years old. We were drastically different, and we had our own lives. Time has a way of moving on without us really noticing.

After her diagnosis, Wendy sent me a friend request on Facebook and we built a tentative relationship. Visiting her in Vancouver, where she was receiving treatment, is something I will always be glad I did. We sat on her bed and looked at old pictures and laughed about our childhood. She talked to me about having cancer, the medications she was taking, what chemo and radiation were like. Her roommate made us lunch and we all ate together at the table while we laughed and talked. It amazed me how positive Wendy was; how optimistic.

She walked me to my car later and we kissed and hugged each other so tightly. It was the last time I would ever see her. Less than two years later, I was standing at the helm of a boat in the Atlantic reading a text from one sister saying that the other sister was dead. I had now lost two siblings.

There was no funeral for Wendy, no memorial service. We heard that her body had been donated to research. My once-vivacious older sister was simply gone.

***

A friend pointed out to me once that I really only have one option in life - to keep going forward; to sink, or swim. In whatever manner necessary, I just have to keep going. Life is beautiful, and life is also hideously ugly sometimes, yet I feel fortunate that I am the type of person who focuses on the beauty.

My life seems to consist of cycles of falling into the depths of despair, and then rising out of my own ashes and creating something new. It's the reason I can't stay still, the reason I move so often, the reason I run, leaving in my wake the scorched remains of all the mini-lives I've lived. Because, for me, nothing seems to last long. I wonder often, with dread in my heart, if I'll always be like this. People are forever telling me that I'm living a dream life, full of adventure, new places, and wonderful experiences. My darkest secret is that I absolutely despise when people say that to me. They don't see my loneliness, my aloneness, my fear, my over-drawn bank account. They don't see that I'm simply running because I have no idea how to stay still. They see what I want them to see on social media. I've forsaken security for the thrill of living, but as I get older, I realize how fundamentally important financial stability is. It's all fun and games until you find yourself in your 60's working at McDonald's. I keep secret the fact that all I really want is someone to roam with; the right someone. And while I'm happy alone, happiness with someone similar to me, someone as nomadic as me, is something I've always been seeking.

That adventurous, nomadic streak in me is very dominating and powerful. I fear I'll never be able to truly settle down; that I'll forever crave the unsettling feeling of change. I've often wondered if that's what I love about working on boats – the feeling of being off-centered; of having to hang on because at any moment your world could tip. Why do I need that feeling to survive? What is it about me that can't exist without constant change? No one else in my family seems to have that, or maybe they've simply learned to tame it. I do love the way I am, but I worry about my future. I suppose worry is natural, though.

I had a wonderful conversation once on the stern of an old wooden sailboat with a girl from Seattle who's a single mom. I told her that the thought of having children terrifies me and is really the only thing in life that scares me enough to not do it. She said that if I weren't scared, it would mean I wasn't taking it seriously. Maybe the same can be applied to life in general? If I'm nervous and worried about my future, does that mean I'm accepting it for the serious thing it is? Or does that just mean that I'm stressing myself out unnecessarily?

Either way, the fact remains the same that the importance of being financially stable and independent, for me, is becoming something I want to achieve, while still staying true to my nomadic heart. Maybe someday I'll get there. Until then, I'm thankful beyond words for the experiences I've encountered, the memories I have, and the Souvenir Friends I've collected. One day, when my number is called, I'm grateful that I'll be able to look back on my life and pull from the bank of amazing memories and know, without a doubt, that I lived the life I wanted. What more can any of us ask for?

I have found myself home in the Pacific Northwest so many times, a place that has once again become beautiful to me now that the pain in my heart has dissipated. I have gone back to The Boat Company for five seasons, living aboard the Liseron in Ballard, a northern neighborhood of Seattle, supervising a major refit while she's dry docked. The Liseron is always there to catch me when I fall, and The Boat Company seems to always know intuitively when to throw the life ring out to me because I am drowning in my own mistakes. Only a few people knew I was homeless in Massachusetts, living in the parking garage, showering at the YMCA. My stubborn pride held me back from reaching out for help. The night I sought out God, I felt I had no one left to turn to, and so I did something I never have before – I prayed. I cried, and I prayed, and I asked for help.

A few days after moving into the empty apartment, a phone call came from The Boat Company asking if I would consider returning to work for them, living aboard the

Liseron again and doing boat maintenance. While I'll admit that accepting was in fact my only option, it was an option that thrilled me. I love the Liseron. I love and respect The Boat Company, and I deeply missed home, the mystic and dew-drenched Pacific Northwest. It was my saving grace, this request to return to the company. I shudder to think what might have become of me if they hadn't called. This, like so many other experiences in my life, is further proof that everything happens for a reason; that we suffer through tragedy in order to ensure that we fully and truly appreciate the good, because even when there's bad, there's so much good to be thankful for. I believe that with every fiber of my being. Life truly is a beautiful miracle.

Liberty (far left) and her siblings with their biological father, Paul

Liberty with Paul in 2016

Bern Miller 1995

Liberty and Bern as kids on the Oregon Coast

Liberty and Wendy in 2015

Liberty and her parents on the Oregon Coast, 2017

Liberty and her dad, Bruce

Liberty's grandparents, James and Lottie Martin

Essex Street in Salem, Mass

The church across the street from the parking garage in Salem

Liberty with Jared and Melissa

Liberty and Doug ("The Admiral") in Nova Scotia

Chapter Seven

"With your street lamp for a soul, I am just one of many insects in your light" Floater

I've had shallow roots for as long as I can remember. Since I was a tiny girl I've had the feeling of wanting to leave, though I didn't yet have the words to describe it. Maybe as an adult I still don't have the words. I would ride in the backseat of the car, driving along the familiar streets of my hometown, and point out different houses to my parents and say, "let's move there". I have always wanted to just...go.

When I was in the fifth grade my grandparents took me camping on the Oregon Coast. We met a couple who lived in a converted school bus and seemed blissfully happy and in love. It was that moment when I realized that what I was craving was a nomadic lifestyle. Since then I have wanted nothing more than to roam in a bus or van with the man I love; a man who loves me back just as much.

Neither of those things has happened for me – the bus or the man. But the roaming has happened.

When I was in my late teens and early 20's, I couldn't walk into a store alone, and I was too scared to drive the freeway. I would take back roads the 20 or so miles between Wimer and Grants Pass to go to the store. Parking in the vast lot, I would sit in my car and try to find the courage to go into the store alone. At that point in my life, I hadn't done a single thing alone. There was always someone with me, whether it was my mom, a boyfriend, or a friend, I had never been faced with doing something as simple as going shopping alone.

And so, I would sit there, watching the front doors of the store and working up the nerve to walk in. Sometimes, I would walk half way across the parking lot only to turn and rush back to the safety and comfort of my car. Most often, I would drive away without ever having gotten out of the car. It was a horrid feeling of weakness. I was bitterly ashamed of myself for not having the independence and strength of character to do my shopping by myself. I don't remember when that changed, but I remember the feeling of determination to be different.

I've come so far since then and have spent the last nearly ten years roaming the world alone and living in the back of my Jeep Grand Cherokee Laredo. It's not what I imagined as a young girl, but it's beautiful nonetheless.

I've always struggled with meaninglessness. I fear that I will die having accomplished nothing great. I don't want to be like my brother - always dreaming of something beyond where you are but dying before you have half a chance to reach it. This fear, whether irrational or not, has been the cause of my lifelong movement; my constant running, my never-ending quest for the next best thing. I am forever seeking somewhere other than where I am, forever chasing dreams.

***

After my climb to survival from rock bottom in late 2016 and the months that followed when I became an even stronger and happier person than I had ever been, I met the man I wanted to roam with. Or rather, my feelings shifted for a friend I had always adored (remember that dreadlocked kayak guide that my ex used to worry about...oops), and I realized that he was it for me. Our changing feelings for one another was so unexpected and took us both by surprise, but we ran with it and it became the most beautiful thing I've ever experienced with another person. I was terrified. I was beyond terrified, but in my heart and mind and soul, he was beyond worth it.

We met in early 2015 in Friday Harbor, that charming town on the small island in Puget Sound where we both were working as sea kayak guides, though for different companies. The moment I met him, on the sidewalk in front of the Crows Nest coffee shop, I felt my soul come alive. It wasn't a romantic feeling for me, rather a feeling of having found home; of having found something I had spent my whole life looking for and could never seem to find. I instantly and deeply adored him on a level that I have never before and never since felt for anyone (sorry everyone else).

I spent the ensuing summer of new friendship wondering what it was about this person that felt different to me. I would send him random text messages telling him how much I adored him, and I would always find myself feeling nervous when we had plans to meet up, though I still didn't think it was a romantic feeling. It was simply so deep and so profound, and I was struggling to figure out why he felt like the only home I ever wanted to know.

Years of friendship later, I discovered why. We had both moved away from the island but still made a point to keep in touch and see each other when we could, which wasn't often since we're both nomads. It had been a year since we had seen each other, and we had plans to meet in Bellingham for the day.

I was like a kid on Christmas Eve and couldn't sleep the night before. As the hours ticked by, I found myself becoming frustrated and angry at the fact that I felt nervous. Still, I couldn't figure out why my stomach was filled with butterflies at the thought of meeting up with my old buddy.

The next day, the nervousness grew as I sat in the Woods coffee shop on Bay Street in Bellingham waiting for him, and when the doors opened, and he walked toward me with that smile of his lighting up his face and his arms thrown wide and waiting to wrap around me, I finally figured it all out. The realization was like walking into a brick wall. I still don't know why it had taken me so long to realize that what I was feeling for him far exceeded friendship.

As he wrapped me up in his arms and pulled me close, everything in life finally made sense. I was exactly where I wanted to be. I had finally found where I belonged. He was home to me. And that fucking terrified me more than anything ever has.

What he and I shared from that day on was the most gorgeous thing. It was everything I had always wanted but had never seemed able to find. He was everything I had always wanted. It was easy and peaceful and magical and comfortable and right. But he was going away – to Seward, Alaska where he was a seasonal kayak guide.

When I flew to Alaska to visit him, he surprised me by being at the airport when I landed. In that moment, I was overwhelmed that he was there for me. As other travelers and the girls behind the rental car counters watched us laugh and hug and kiss, I was overwhelmed with a feeling of pride, and it was because of him. I had never, not once, been that girl, at an airport or anywhere else, that a man surprises because he simply can't wait another minute to see her. I finally was that girl, and it was the most incredible feeling I've ever known.

We spent the next two weeks camping in the downpour of Alaskan rain; laughing and talking and holding one another so tightly within the confines of the tent walls. He introduced me to his friends and co-workers and roommates. We went kayaking on Resurrection Bay and paddleboarding in an iceberg-filled lagoon at the face of a tidewater glacier. While he was at work, I hung out at his house with his friends like I had always been a part of it, because, for the first time in my life, I felt as if I belonged.

Of all the places I've lived and all the people I've called friends, I've never truly felt like I belonged. I've always existed just on the outskirts, though I'm excellent at pretending that I don't feel that way. I'm usually always the first to leave the party, because even though I'm having a blast and I'm a social person, I'm also a solitary person. More often than not, I would rather be alone, parked in my car somewhere or aboard my boat where I can quietly contemplate life. I'm the classic extroverted introvert. But this time, in Seward with him and his people, I finally...belonged.

From the day I met him on the island in 2015, I was reminded of my brother. He was everything I imagined Bern would have been, had he lived. He seemed to feel a connection with my brother as well, and after we became close, he would tell me how thoughts of my brother consumed his mind while he was out kayaking. He said pretty words to me – that my brother would be proud of the woman I had become. They were words that meant more to me than I think he realized, and words that hurt me most of all in the end, because I question if he truly meant them.

In the 20 years since my brother died, I've had only four dreams of him. These dreams have spanned the years, leaving me waiting for the next one.

The first one happened about a year after Bern was killed, and in it, he was walking away from me down a dusty road. I screamed his name, but he never turned around. In the two dreams since, I've seen a bit more of his face each time, but never clearly, and only a bit of his profile.

I've waited so patiently for the dream when I finally can see his full face. I had that dream in Seward.

My brother stood before me smiling, staring into my eyes, and nodding his head up and down. Standing next to me was my kayak guide that I so deeply adored. I've always wondered what it meant that he was in the dream I so desperately longed for. And I've wondered why it seems that he and my brother, whom he never met, have such a deep connection.

And so, when he asked me to move to Seward, I did. I flew home, quit my kayak instructing job, got in my Jeep and drove five days along the Alcan Highway, solo, from Bellingham, Washington to Seward, Alaska. Four days after I got to Seward, things ended between us. He was honest about not wanting to be in a "labeled" relationship, and I was honest about wanting a committed partner. We couldn't give each other what we needed, so we both walked away. Even though I wanted him in my life, I knew it was important to stick to my resolve and believe in the fact that I knew I deserved someone who wasn't afraid to commit. I wasn't asking for marriage. I wasn't asking for children. I don't want either of those things. And I wasn't trying to tame his wildness. All I wanted from him was a person to share my time with; a person to laugh with, to roam with. A person who made me happy, for however long it lasted, because I've never believed in "till death do us part". Life is long, and people change. I believe in, "until we no longer make each other happy". I just wasn't expecting that it would come so soon for him.

Nonetheless, I felt that he abandoned me in a town where all the people I knew, were his people. He never messaged to ask if I was okay living in my car – if I was warm enough, if I was safe. But one of the things I always liked most about him when we were together was that he never worried about me. The one thing I dislike about nearly everyone, is that their concern for my lifestyle borders on pity. I've chosen this life. I've chosen to be a nomad and live in my Jeep. And I love this life.

As the shock of his instantaneous change of heart wore off, I began to realize that I didn't really feel anything at all, but not in a way that meant I didn't have very real and very deep feelings for him. I cried for him only once, and that's a first for me. It was nearly as if the pain ran so deep that I couldn't even feel it, whereas usually the pain is so close to the surface, so superficial, that it's all I can do to keep it from overflowing. But he was different. In every possible way. He was exactly what I wanted, and somehow, I lost it. One of my wonder woman abilities has always been the fierce desire to succeed in the face of disappointment. It's as if heartbreak ignites an inferno within me that won't be tamed unless I get my revenge via thriving.

So now, even though he's just another chapter in my book, he was, and will always be, so much more than that. He was the greatest one in my life. Greater than all of them combined. Maybe he doesn't deserve that title, but then again, maybe he does. Without knowing it and without even trying, he has always made me want to be a better person, even when we shared only friendship. Having him in my life made me want to grow, and I feel as if I'll always draw inspiration from the memory of his friendship. Sharing time with him healed so many of my old wounds and opened a beautiful part of my heart that I never knew existed. I'm very grateful for that experience because before him, I had never known that feeling of finding home with any man; I had never known that I even wanted that feeling.

Chapter Eight

"While you are warm and safe, just think of us shivering, beautifully brave, black sheep who've formed a pack" Floater

"Do you think we're addicted to the chaos that our nomadic lifestyle brings?" Corbin asked as we sat under a tree at the park overlooking Resurrection Bay in Seward, Alaska.

We were sitting on our backpacks in the wet grass while rain dripped from the leaves above our heads, passing one fork between us while we practically inhaled an amazing piece of cheesecake from Zudy's Café.

His words resonated deeply within my soul and I paused with my hand halfway between my mouth and the container he was holding, the fork loaded with chocolate and caramel goodness. I gazed out at the steel-grey water, boats coming and going and kayakers bowing their heads against the biting wind and then I looked into Corbin's eyes. "Fuck yes, I do".

It's become the motto that he and I share – "addicted to the chaos". We still say it to each other so often. It is undoubtedly an addiction. I crave change. I thrive on the act of leaving. I am so accustomed to being alone that I don't think I really know how to be with someone for a decent length of time, though I want to share my life with a man who truly loves me.

As our conversation progressed and we began scraping the bottom of the cheesecake container, we spoke of the fact that, though the lifestyle we've chosen is difficult, we wouldn't trade it, change it, or give it up for anything. Even when things are scary hard, and they are often scary hard when you're a nomad, we wouldn't have it any other way. Because our lives are extraordinary. We understand this. And it's what makes us bond. The challenges we choose and the hardships we share - it's all a choice. And it's a beautiful choice.

I spent the summer of 2017 living in Seward in the back of my Jeep. My car has always been my one consistent home and I feel such gratitude to own it. I would park by Exit Glacier each night and sit in the driver's seat listening to music while writing in my journal and gazing out at the glacier-fed river. Eventually, I would crawl between the front seats into my little bed in the back and listen to the river rushing by as it polished ancient stones with its powerful force. I would count the fat, ever-present rain drops as they splashed like tears from the sky onto the metal roof of the Jeep.

My summer in Seward was very profound for me; a beautiful challenge. I solo drove the Alcan Highway through Washington, British Columbia, the Yukon, and Alaska, with hopes and dreams guiding my way. Those hopes and the plans I had made with another person didn't work out, and that's okay. I have always strongly believed that everything happens for a reason; that life works out the way it's meant to, even if it's drastically different than what we had imagined. I believe that every person comes into our lives when they're meant to, and that they leave our lives when they're meant to. And I had made a promise to myself to never allow my feelings for a man destroy me again. I intended to keep that promise.

Even though I hadn't intended to move to Alaska, I was absolutely meant to go there that summer. I went up for someone I believed in; someone I had so much faith in, and after the initial disappointment, and feeling foolishly like another notch in his kayak paddle, I remembered my beliefs, and I stopped feeling sorry for myself. I began to see the lessons and the beauty. I wasn't meant to go to Seward for him – I was meant to go to Seward for ME, and for all the beautiful souls I connected with while I was there. Had I not gone, I never would have met Corbin or Jackie or Libby or Bryan or Mere or any of the wonderful friends from the Czech Republic that I spent all summer working with at the Sea Bean Café, a place where, for the second time in my life, I felt instantly welcomed and loved and accepted. I never would have had the beautifully challenging summer that I did; a summer that forced me to look deeply within myself and see things I had buried long ago.

Working at the Sea Bean Café was a random accident, though nothing in life is ever really an accident. Within a matter of days after deciding that I would move to Alaska and take a leap of faith for love, I met a girl in Seward who was quitting her barista position at the Sea Bean. It seemed to be divine providence. I was a trained barista and needed a job. A few days later I spoke to the owners and they offered me the position.

From the moment I walked into the Sea Bean, I felt like it was right; like I was where I was supposed to be. My co-workers welcomed me with such open arms that it nearly hurt; to feel so immediately loved after having been so deeply hurt and disappointed by another person was salve for my wounds.

The café participated in the J1 program – a visa for foreign nationals attending college and needing practical training to complete their degrees. This meant that a good portion of my co-workers were from the Czech Republic. With staff housing in the back of the café (I got hired too late in the season and all the housing was full), it truly was a family environment. Never have I worked somewhere that felt like a loving home. Though the café was hectic with cruise ship passengers, we were able to create a working atmosphere that was genuinely fun, and at night we would gather in the hallway of the staff house, sitting on the floor with our backs against the walls, laughing and talking.

I felt so grateful to have found a café filled with wonderful people. They were my reason for staying in Seward. I've always been so good at leaving. When things didn't turn out as I had expected in Seward, I nearly left. I had only been working at the café for two days when things unraveled with the dude I moved up there for. It would have been so easy to leave, but for one of the first times in my life, I didn't want to leave. I think that scared me more than anything – that desire to stay. After two days I already loved the café and loved my co-workers. And I had loved Seward since the first time I saw it, fourteen years earlier.

So, I stayed, and because I stayed I met my people – the people with whom I felt I belonged with.

There were four of us that were homeless. I met them because they would hang out at the café when they weren't at work at various restaurants around town. I met Corbin first. He was friends with Bryan, the cook at the Sea Bean. Corbin is one of those people that I immediately clicked with. We were both homeless, lost, a bit scared, but wild-eyed with excitement, and both Pisces.

When Corbin introduced me to Ashley and Matty, we became the four homeless kids of Seward. Everyone else had staff housing – we had tents and hammocks and cars. We peed outside and showered at the marina and froze our asses off at night. Matty would sit in the armchair in the corner window of the café, put on his sunglasses, prop his phone up in his hand on his leg, and sleep. It was classic. To everyone else, it looked like he was just addicted to his iPhone, but all of us who worked at the Sea Bean knew that he was sleeping after long cold nights in the park. When we noticed him starting to stir, we would make his usual coffee and put it on the table beside him. We took care of each other. We had each other's backs and did what we could to help one another. We truly were a family and I felt so grateful to be a part of it.

The family I made in Seward was the most beautiful part of my whole summer. I am so glad that I stayed for them. Even though we've all now left Alaska for the winter, we still talk on a regular basis. And by talk, I mean we actually call each other on the phone. Like true family.

As I stood at the espresso machine one day, Jackie, the baker at the café, handed me an orange plastic squirt gun with a little piece of paper taped to it. I took it, looking at her questioningly. "Assassin", she said. "The name of your target is written on the paper."

Jackie had organized a game of Assassin, in which we all had secret targets and our mission was to take them out with the squirt gun, with the café being the safe zone. We spent weeks being jumpy and suspicious of one another in the most fun way. We stalked one another around town and pretended to die dramatically when we were hit.

As I made coffee for a customer one afternoon, my target, Noah, walked out the back door of the café into the alley. I handed the milk pitcher to Eva to finish steaming it, tip-toed down the hall of the staff house, peeked my head out the door to find my target, and then chased Noah down the alley while we both laughed and hooted and hollered. Cornering himself, Noah died with dignity behind a trash can from multiple squirt gun shots to the chest.

Because of that summer, I found myself in a position of self-reflection and self-discovery. I was so happy that I stayed in Seward instead of running away like I always did. And because I stayed I found something gorgeous – I found people that I belong with.

I've always been solo. Even when I was married I was solo. By the time I found myself in Seward in the summer of 2017, I had reached a point of such fierce independence that I would protect my adventures from intruders. I didn't want anyone else to join in on my fun; I wanted to take cross-country road trips alone, and move to new towns alone, and have all kinds of adventures and experiences alone. I'm a loner; I always have been, even as a child. Yet I'm also very social. But I become exhausted so quickly from being around people.

But Seward was different for me. I still spent a lot of time alone in my car, but I spent more time hanging at the staff house and having bonfires on the beach and sweating my booty off at weekly dance party at the Yukon Bar.

On one of my very few days off from the café, I planned to drive the couple hours north to Anchorage to run errands. As I sat at the café with the rest of the homeless kids, I casually mentioned my Anchorage plans for the next day. It was Corbin's day off as well, and he asked if he could come with me. I hesitated, because I wanted to go alone. I don't know why I wanted to go alone, I just did, because that's what I do. But instead I said yes, that he could join me, and it turned out to be one of the best days I had all summer.

We talked the entire drive to Anchorage; deep talk, not superficial. We stopped at the Alaska Wildlife Conservation Center and watched wolves sleep in the rain and bears scratch themselves on logs. As we drove around Anchorage running errands, we passed the tattoo shop where Jackie and I had gotten piercings a few weeks before. Corbin and I looked at each other for a few seconds, and I pulled into the parking lot. We spent the next few hours getting tattooed. On a whim, because that's how we live our lives. Addicted to the chaos.

Later, as we watched people ice skate at the mall, we psyched ourselves up for skinny dipping in Portage Lake. We blasted music on the drive along the Seward Highway, and kept singing as we stopped and got coffee at the gas station in Girdwood. By the time we got to Portage Lake and dipped a toe in, we both decided that we were fucking crazy to even consider taking our clothes off in the frigid Alaska night air, and even crazier to jump into a lake fed by a glacier.

We got back in the Jeep and blasted the heater along with the music. Two minutes down the road, the most majestic bull moose blocked our path. With the daylight waning and the alpenglow setting the Chugach Mountains ablaze, we sat silently and basked in the beauty of nature. The moose watched us as well, and then dipped into the

141

forest and was gone. Again, Corbin and I simply looked at each other.

The day I left Seward was one of the most difficult I've experienced. I'm usually ready to leave, but this time I didn't feel I was, but my "big girl" job with The Boat Company aboard the Liseron was waiting for me in Seattle. I cried openly that day, something that is very rare for me. So many people came to the café to tell me goodbye. Everyone except the one who mattered most, at least in the beginning, the one I ended up in Seward because of.

I can't tell you why my summer in Seward changed me. All I can tell you is that it did. Perhaps it was because I felt I had found exactly what I had always been looking for – another soul who was so profound to me that it filled every dark corner of my heart with a radiant light like I have never known before. My greatest fear is that I will never again encounter something that beautiful.

The Admiral says he feels that I grew up in Seward; that I learned so much about myself and my inner needs and desires that I can no longer go back to the person I was not even one year ago. I believe he's right. Having experienced what I've always longed for, and somehow losing that thing that felt so destined, changed me in ways that even I don't understand. Maybe I never will understand it. But it forced me to not only look within, but to give myself permission to bring those internal lessons to the surface; to finally set boundaries and live my life on my terms – not the terms that everyone else thinks I should live by.

Without even being fully aware of it, I began to manifest and express those boundaries, and it took me by surprise when people respected them. However, not everyone respected them – and not everyone approved of them. I lost several good friends once I was back home in Bellingham because of these new boundaries. But I see now that they were one-sided friendships; friends who needed me in order to feel whole, not friends who were complete on their own. And though my life is more peaceful without those friendships, sometimes I'm overcome with such a feeling of guilt because in those people's minds, I hurt them, and feeling like you've hurt someone is unsettling. But I'm more of myself without them; more settled and not stretched as thin by their constant need for me to fix them or save them. Every person is responsible for saving themselves, but some people don't want to be saved. I learned that a long time ago, when people were trying to save me, and I fought them at every turn. It wasn't until I felt truly ready that I began to save myself.

Chapter Nine

"Your whole life, you've been softly fading. Once you were strong, but now degrading, and searching for a light to lead the way" Floater

Isn't it interesting how one seemingly insignificant thing can change the course of your entire life?

Nearly two years ago I was living on the east side of Lake Whatcom in Bellingham, Washington. Life was not good. I was working full-time at a minimum wage job in a coffee shop and part-time as a kayak instructor (which I adored), money was non-existent, rent was expensive, and I was in a bad relationship with a guy who drank all our money away and I wasn't quite sure how to remove myself from the unhappy situation.

As I drove home one day, winding my way along the banks of the lake, I noticed a yard sale sign. Yard sales have never really been my thing, but this sign boasted "lots of kayaks", and kayaks definitely were my thing.

As I wandered around the yard sale I got to talking with the man hosting it. We geeked out on kayaks and it was brought to my attention that he was the founder of Ocean Kayak, and the inventor of the sit-on-top kayak. We exchanged information and that was that.

Not quite one year later, when I was out of the bad relationship and home in the Pacific Northwest after living in Salem, Mass, I found myself in the throes of starting my own kayaking company. I rummaged through my storage unit one rainy day and found that business card. And then I called him, Tim Niemier, a name that is nearly legend in the worldwide kayaking community.

We met at Woods Coffee in Bellingham's Barkley Village, and as they say, the rest is history. I now find myself typing this book while sitting at the bar in Tim's kitchen, looking out over the Pacific Ocean from a small island off Vancouver Island's west coast.

But Tim isn't here. He's home in Bellingham. I'm here alone, on the island that Tim own's, in the house that Tim built with his own hands nearly 45 years ago. I'm spending the month of January caretaking that house. I am completely and utterly alone on this 60 acre island that is so remote it's not even on the map. I sit watching the tide come and go, the harbor seals splash and forage, and the eagles chatter from the tree tops.

I've spent nearly my whole life on my own, but this is the first time that I am truly alone. I agreed to this caretaking position because since returning home from Seward I've felt overwhelmed by people, and telling the same story over and over about my transformation was making me edgy. Most people don't seem to understand why Seward changed me, and I can't find the words to explain it to them. Like I said, I don't know why it changed me, but it did. And now here I am, in self-imposed isolation, on an island in Canada trying to put my life and my feelings into words. I struggle to convey the roiling mass of chaos that lingers inside. I often wonder if I'm the only one who feels so lost, and so baffled by life and overwhelmed by its profoundness and its beauty.

Nearly daily people tell me that I'm living their dream life, or that they're living vicariously through me. And while I realize that my life via social media is an adventure-packed nomadic dream, that's unfortunately not the entire reality of it. I post photos of the many different places I spend time, the amazing experiences I have, and the extraordinary people I encounter along the way. I don't, however, post photos of the times I cry in the back of my Jeep because I am so lost and so alone. I don't proclaim to the world of Instagram how confused I feel. Instead, I portray what I don't always feel – strength and bravery. I live by the adage of 'fake it till you make it." I just haven't made it yet.

I seem to have within me this entirely fucked up inability to stay, especially when something goes wrong. So, I go. I go because I have the freedom to do so (not the financial freedom, but the no kids/no career freedom). I have the desire to go and do and explore and discover and experience. But deep down, the root of why I am the way I am, is because I hadn't found my place until I went to Seward, and though I have found my people, I still haven't found my person.

I'm always on the lookout for something different, something better, and sometimes I despise being that way because it means that I always end up living in the back of my car in a place where I don't really know anyone. It means that I've gambled all my pennies away on one machine, and that machine just crapped out and ate my money. And it usually means that my heart is broken. Again. To some degree at least. Though I've become nearly numb to devastation.

But it also means that I'm someplace rad; someplace beautiful that is filled with memories to be made and friends to connect with. Every time Corbin and I talk on the phone it's usually always the same – that we feel lost and alone, but that we absolutely adore our lives. I'm an advocate for living in a way that you love, no matter what society tells us, no matter how many times your family asks you when you're going to "settle down". For people like me, there is no such thing as settling down. It's not even an option.

People email asking how I became a nomad, and how they can become one, too. I'm brutally honest with them and list all the difficult challenges of living the way I do. In Seward, I washed my socks and underwear in a glacier fed stream and then hung them to dry in the back of the Jeep, usually forgetting to take them down before someone got into my car (don't mind my thong hanging there...), I showered once a week – if I was lucky. Before I made friends (and sometimes even after I made friends) I would sit in my car staring out the window for a while because I had nowhere to go and no one to hang out with. I slept in my car while worrying about being raped and/or murdered. I peed outside more often than I peed in a toilet. I could never find anything I was looking for, though I knew it was in the Jeep somewhere. I never had money. And forget using the "wanna come back to my place?" line.

My nomadic life means that I am always the girl who's leaving. I'm always the girl who's alone. You think my life is filled with adventure and bravery. You think I have freedom. You see my lifestyle as romantic. It's all about perspective, and not believing everything you read. And still, I find this life beautiful beyond words, and tell those who ask me for advice about changing their life that it is full of unimaginable sacrifice, and unimaginable fulfillment.

Instagram, and #vanlife, have created within our society a corrupt assumption that travel is glamorous (and sure, it can be); that those of us who are active nomads live this blissfully carefree lifestyle (only sometimes). But I'll let you in on a secret....travel is brutal and unforgiving. It's heartbreaking, sometimes via the world's beauty and sometimes because the world shatters you into pieces, it's oftentimes scary, especially when you solo-travel like I do, it's expensive, it's time-consuming and, for me personally, it leaves me feeling alone and lonely and viciously alive, all at the same time.

Sometimes I think back to the life I used to have, that suffocating "American Dream", and I feel my heart and soul swell with gratitude that I got out. And these days, the American Dream is changing. Now it seems that everyone wants to live in their car and travel, something that my nomad friends and I have been doing since #BeforeItWasCool.

For me, travel is an addiction, a drug, a necessity; it's something I crave, something I must have in order to survive. And just like any junkie, it's something that I've destroyed relationships over and given up good careers for. There have been times when I've walked out on everything and everyone so I could have my next adventure. Being a traveler has forced me to make brutal choices between my wanderlust and my stability and time and again, I've chosen my wanderlust. Sometimes, when I am lost in the wilderness of chaos, I curse my nomadic soul. But only sometimes. And it never lasts long.

Even when you speak with the greatest humility about your travels, there's still that look, that judgment. And it comes in all forms. There's the person who assumes that you simply are not keen on getting a 'real' job and therefore choose to run from responsibility (ie: the corporate job) and hide in the far corners of the world. There's the person who figures you must be a trust fund baby because how else could you afford to travel, the person who thinks you're homeless, the person who has you pegged as a commitment-phob and then, worst of all, there's the person who lets their envy turn to bitterness.

Even when I've stuffed my tales down into the depths of my being and not mentioned a peep about them, I've had my gypsyhood destroy friendships with women who were held firmly, and a bit reluctantly, in the grips of motherhood. Them simply looking at the map on my living room wall with all those little pins on all those destinations was enough to crush our friendship.

But I also have those friends who are extraordinarily proud of me for living the way I do; the ones who display my postcards on their living room walls like my very dear friend Teresa in my hometown, the ones who tell me that I inspire them. Each positive comment fills my heart and reminds me that I truly am living my best version of life, and I have so many people who support me, and encourage me, and love me.

Being a nomad is an unforgiving, soul-consuming way of life that tests the relationships I encounter and the bonds I create. Having that jittery need to escape, to go and see and do and truly live, is oftentimes a burden. The hardest part of traveling, for me, is saying goodbye. Yet I've chosen to embrace that burden and turn it into something gorgeous, whatever that may be. I would rather spend the rest of my life crying as I drive away then never having known the beauty that is out there in the world. And damn, this world is beautiful. It's worth all the sacrifices I've made and will continue to make.

Epilogue

Writing has been such an important part of my life since I was old enough to do it. When I was young, I used to write letters to my mom was I was mad at her. Words on paper were the only way I felt able to truly express my emotions.

I used to envy how articulate my brother was when he was mad. He would rage and scream things that sounded so profound to me; things that made so much sense and resonated with me. There have been times in my life when I've wished that I could be good at fighting with spoken words. It's a bizarre thing to wish for, but when I'm upset, my voice fails me, so I write, yet writing this book was very difficult for me. I could only write small sections at a time as the heaviness of the way I grew up, and the things that happened would begin to weigh on me. It's taken me 20 years to finish writing this book, but I felt it was a story that needed to be told; my hope is that other people out there who are struggling will be inspired by these words and believe that becoming a strong, independent person, despite the pain, or maybe because of it, is entirely an option. I've consciously chosen to live a happy life, even when life has seemed intent on defeating me.

This earth is an amazing place, and life is a stunning and incredible gift. I will be forever grateful that I was strong enough to make that difficult decision to change and leave behind the life I knew to see the world and live the life I wanted. I can't describe how the experiences I've had, the people I've met, and the places I've seen have changed me; I have a new-found respect and understanding of nearly everything. I believe to my very core that travel is the greatest form of education. The people I've encountered have each had a profound effect on me and I will cherish the memory of their faces until the day I die. I've traveled the world alone. I've slept on the couches and floors of strangers. I've walked foreign cities at night in the rain. I've seen humanity at its worst, and I've also seen it at its best. I've loved deeply, and I've been deeply hurt. My tears have been brought on by both sadness and unbelievable joy. And I will always, ALWAYS, be grateful for every single second of my life. I'm a changed person, but I will always be that person that gives everything to whatever it is I'm passionate about. Sometimes that's a good thing and sometimes that's a bad thing, but it's who I am.

And I will tell you this: nearly every day reminds me that life is worth living, and although at times it feels so incredibly bleak, there is always something amazing to be found if your eyes are wide open. Being alive is not a thing to be wasted.

Life won't wait, and neither should you, because someday never comes.

Journals

Below are my personal journals that I kept while at the Cove in Taiji, Japan and aboard the Steve Irwin in the Mediterranean.

They are my own thoughts and opinions and should not be used to base judgment upon the Sea Shepherd Conservation Society, nor any of the individuals involved in the organization. I've intentionally removed the last names of SSCS "higher-ups" out of respect.

The Cove:

November 1, 2010

Here I sit, 30,000 feet in the air, on a very turbulent plane. I can't believe I'm on my way to Japan; on my way to the famed Cove. When the documentary came out, I never dreamed I would one day be going there. It all has happened so fast. Everyone has been incredibly supportive, and most are completely in awe that I'm doing this. It's amazing even to me. Who would have thought that I'd be doing something like this? This is perfectly and exactly my dream. I'm actively helping protect dolphins via my photography and writing. I can't even begin to find the words for what this trip means to me. I quit my photography career and am flying 12 hours away from everything I know simply to help save dolphins. And I wouldn't change it for the world. I am 100% confident in the decisions I've made that have led me to this very seat on this very plane. This is what I was meant to do. This is what I was born to do.

I know I'll get a lot emotionally out of this trip, especially considering that divorce has come knocking at my door, but I'm also hoping that it will perhaps open doors for me that might not have opened otherwise. But ultimately, who knows what will come of this. If I end up back in Bellingham next week, back at Grizzly Industrial, photographing sandpaper and drill bits again, I'll still have a phenomenal experience to occupy my mind while I trudge through the rat race. But this trip, this experience and these things I'm going to see, they're going to change me. Next week, I'll be a different person because of the sights my eyes will behold; because of witnessing dolphin slaughter.

November 5, 2010

Only a few days have passed since I've written, yet it feels like months. I feel so emotionally exhausted and even though we've been starting our days at 3:15am, the physical exhaustion is nothing compared to the mental and emotional numbness. Yesterday the fishermen drove an estimated 177 bottlenose dolphins into the Cove. They were done netting them off by about noon and then came to the Cove to watch us watch the dolphins. They sit up on the road, against the railing, watching us. Yet here we are, watching them.

Today we began just shortly after 3am, and now it's 7:30pm. I feel like I've been awake for years. My mind is so tired that writing is proving to be a challenge, but I know that I absolutely must document this chapter of my life.

The dolphin trainers came into the Cove today and, in all, 37 dolphins were selected for captivity, to be sent to the various reaches of the globe for life in an aquarium. They were bottlenose, Flipper dolphins, so each one fetched a price of several hundred thousand dollars. The rest were driven into the killing cove, away from where we could easily see them, to spend their second night with a net between them and the sea. Tomorrow, the remaining 140 will be slaughtered.

It was so unreal to stand there and watch those selected dolphins being dragged out by boats, on slings attached to the side of the skiff. One of the Cove Guardians captured footage of a trainer beating a dolphin during the selection process. He was in the water selecting dolphins and was knocked over. He punched the dolphin in the face. There was a baby hauled up and flung into the bottom of the skiff and taken over to the sea pens in the Taiji harbor. It will never see its family again.

Tomorrow, I watch my first slaughter...

November 6, 2010

It's just before 4am. We're all meeting in the lobby at 4:15 to be at the Cove by 4:30. Today, the fishermen will slaughter roughly 140 dolphins. My position will be at the top of Takababe, a hill with a vantage point into the killing cove. I'm nearly sick at the thought of what I will witness today. Today will change my life. I'm meant to leave Japan soon, but I have to stay. I just can't leave now. To think of going back to my meaningless life in Bellingham makes my heart hurt.

It's now 3pm. I stood upon the hill today with two of my fellow Cove Guardians while dolphins screamed. The water first ran brown, and it was difficult to tell if it was blood or sediment stirred from thrashing dolphins. The Cove Guardians on the beach couldn't see the death; their vantage point was of a group of dolphins being released. That's all they saw, and they cheered. They were cheering and clapping for the released dolphins, oblivious to the slaughter the three of us were being subjected to, and it was beyond fucked up. While we stood with hidden tears and broken hearts, each happy shout of those who were completely clueless pierced our dark moment and made it even blacker.

The dolphin hunters had tarps pulled over the upper edge of the killing cove, so we didn't know at first that the dolphins were being killed. The fishermen were in the water trying to catch them, which was proving difficult. They would tie a rope to their tails and haul them alongside the skiff. We could see the dolphins thrashing in fear and hitting the sides of the boat. It was so painfully loud. The fisherman would hand the line from the skiff to the man under the tarps, and we could see the dolphins being dragged into the shallows, backward under the tarps. Once there was enough blood, the water turned from brown to red. I've never seen anything like it. Scarlet plumes overtaking the sea water. The dolphins were floating, belly up, dead bodies bumping into each other with the movement of unsettled water.

The large gutting barge appeared at the entrance to the main cove and a skiff began dragging bodies from the killing cove to the barge. They were dragging the bodies three at a time along the side of the skiffs with blue tarps thrown over them. The sea around the barge ran red and blood was literally pouring from the scuppers of the boat. The gutted dolphins were transferred from the barge to a banger boat and taken to the warehouse, closer to Taiji Town, to cut and package the meat. Two of the gutters on the barge were young girls.

At 4:30 this morning, when it was still pitch black, as I headed up to the top of Takababe Hill with two other Cove Guardians, our flashlights turned off so as not to be noticed, one of the dolphin hunters rounded the corner with a flashlight, coming down off the hill. He stood in the middle of the path, blocking our way and telling us "no". One of the Guardians stepped off the path to walk around him and was pushed into the bushes on the hillside. In the exchanges of shoves, the fisherman fell. He lay on his back, screaming into the night air and dialing his cell phone. Six more fishermen showed up and surrounded us. One of the Guardians handed me his video camera, on a tri-pod, and told me to stay behind him, but to continue filming, and to run if he was overpowered. The white rubber boots of the fishermen flashed in the moonlight and our flashlights glinted off the blades of their knives. Frightened by the video camera and the knowledge that this footage would ultimately end up online, the dolphin hunters retreated, and soon the police were there. We showed the police the footage proving that we had not been aggressive toward the fishermen and the decision was made by the police to let the issue rest. Fishermen and Cove Guardians all walked away and proceeded to go about what they had set out to do that day: to slaughter, and to protest.

Today was just a horrific day, and I can't stop seeing in my mind what I saw with my eyes earlier. I'll forever remember the sight of dolphins with their stomachs split open and their insides staining red the deck of the gutting barge.

We went out to dinner tonight in Kii-Katsuura, the town about 15 minutes from Taiji where we stay, and an old man began yelling at us in Japanese from across the restaurant. The woman serving us shushed him and set another beer in front of him. He finally got up and stormed out. I don't like being hated, but it seems that's all Sea Shepherd brings. Hate. They're very different from what you see on TV and social media. There's a dark vein that courses through the organization, and I'm seeing large amounts of that darkness the more involved with them I become.

I'm sorry, I literally can't think anymore. I'm so tired.

November 8, 2010

I've extended my plane ticket. I'm here for another two weeks.

Another large pod was driven into the Cove today. Tomorrow will be a kill day.

I went down to the Cove about 8pm tonight with several other Guardians. It was black as night, but the police were still there. They stay all night when there are dolphins in the Cove, waiting to be slaughtered. We sat upon the sea wall, overlooking the cove, and talked with one of the police officers. He showed us pictures of his kids on his iPhone, with whom he was texting while we sat talking. I was struck by the sadness of it all - him being away from his family because of our protest. He told us that he doesn't believe in killing dolphins and wishes the slaughter would stop.

November 10, 2010

Emotions were running high yesterday. The fishermen slaughtered about 40 dolphins. They tried to release two juveniles, but they kept swimming back into the cove where their mothers were. The fishermen kept trying to drive them out, chasing them out to sea with the banger boats, but they wouldn't leave. Both the mothers were dead, but the juveniles still wouldn't go. They ended up being killed right alongside their mothers.

A roof of blue tarps was put up on the gutting barge. All we could see was the dolphins being transferred from the skiffs to the barge. Then a wave of red spilled out through the scuppers of the barge and stained the sea. All of the Guardians are feeling quite helpless and angry these days. Dolphins keep dying while we stand here and watch. Everyone is wound so tightly, and we wait with bated breath for something to break.

The Cove Guardians have taken to calling the dolphin hunters "molesters". What a fucked up term. It's embarrassing that they insist on calling them that. I'm the only one who doesn't use that term. It's hard to retain my faith and belief in Sea Shepherd when I see daily how childish and petty they can be.

Friends and family have begun sharing my story with anyone who will listen, it seems. I keep receiving emails from people that begin with "you don't know me, but I'm friends with..." The onslaught of support and encouragement has been quite overwhelming in such a beautiful way. It makes me feel like I'm not completely crazy for quitting my job and moving to Japan on a moment's notice to witness dolphin death. However, the one person whom I wish were showing support and isn't, is my husband. We've barely communicated since I've been here, and when we do, it's about practical things such as where the checkbook is kept or what the password is to pay our mortgage online. I've given up hoping that he will understand why I'm here; I've stopped wishing that he will be proud of me and supportive of my beliefs. But I also understand that this just isn't his thing – he has no interest in protecting the oceans, and I have no desire to force that belief upon him.

November 12, 2010

Where do I begin? This has been a wild experience. So many dolphins have been slaughtered since my arrival in Japan. 12 pilot whales were killed yesterday. The most difficult part of it all, for me, is the captivity aspect. We followed one of the trucks that was taking captives to Dolphin Base, where the trainers work with them and train them for aquariums. They had two dolphins in the back of the truck and we were able to walk right up to them. My heart broke a little more with each squeal and thrash. I've been having such a difficult time dealing with the guilt of not being able to help them. Still, days later, the guilt nearly overwhelms me. The wooden crates they put them in to be shipped to aquariums around the world are horrid little boxes. Lined with blue tarps, they cover the dolphin inside with ice and sedate it. These dolphins will spend an average of 20 hours in the crate aboard a truck or an airplane, oftentimes both, before they reach their destination.

I was meant to go home on the 9th, but when the time came to leave, I couldn't. I know my husband will be upset, but I simply cannot image going home now, home to no job and a lonely marriage. I feel in my soul that I need to be here. I can't imagine leaving this place and re-entering the 'real' world. Having seen the terror and devastation of what happens here, my problems seem so trivial. It's shocking how quickly and deeply you bond with someone, a mere stranger, when you witness tragedy together. I just can't imagine not being with these people every day, these Cove Guardians who have become my soul mates. If only I felt this way about my husband. But my life in Bellingham seems like a lifetime ago. My mind is so numb. All this killing has brought up feelings about my brother's death and it's been hard to process it all. This is an experience which I will forever hold dear to my heart. I am still in awe of the support we receive from around the world. It would feel pointless to continue to stand vigil if it weren't for the emails that pour in from supporters claiming that we're making a difference. Those emails nearly restore my faith in humanity. There most definitely are good, caring, kind-hearted people in this world.

November 14, 2010

Life is so bizarre; I just can't comprehend it sometimes. I've spent years being friends with people who I really wouldn't miss if they weren't in my life any longer. But these people here, the other Cove Guardians, are so profoundly important to me. And in such a short amount of time. Two months ago, my life was so different. I can't imagine going back to that deeply lonely life.

November 16, 2010

Yesterday, the fishermen killed a baby dolphin, maybe a couple of weeks old. My position was up in Tsunami Park, overlooking the gutting barge. I'm still in shock over what I saw. When I remember all the blood, it makes my stomach turn. I feel such a heavy depression weighing on me.

Sea Shepherd wants me to stay on for the remainder of the season as the Campaign Leader. The current Campaign Leader is heading home due to a near-expired visa. I want to stay. I want to stay away from my unhappy life at home and do something that I'm passionate about. I've sent my husband an email; I don't want to fight on the phone with him, and I've always been able to explain myself better via writing. I've asked him to take a few days before he responds with a hurtful email. I don't know what this will mean for my marriage, or what exactly I want this to mean for my marriage.

November 19, 2010

I'm in the Kansai (Osaka) airport, heading home to Seattle. Sea Shepherd has booked my return flight to Japan for

December 3, coming home to the States on March 1, 2011. I'll be there three months. I'm so very happy to be going back, and as Campaign Leader. I'll spend the next two weeks home in Bellingham preparing for my return to Japan. My husband's email shocked me. He was very supportive and told me he thinks I need to be in Japan to help the dolphins. I'm hopeful that this is the beginning of the support I've wanted him to show me all the years we've been together.

Yesterday was the most difficult day in Japan so far. It was a brutal kill. They piled the bodies from the Cove into the bottom of the skiffs and covered them with tarps. The fishermen sat upon the dead mound during the transfer to the barge. As I held my position on Tsunami Hill, a skiff came from the whale museum, located in the next cove over from the killing cove, and approached the barge. Two captive dolphins that had been selected from an earlier drive had become depressed in their tank at the whale museum and wouldn't perform. They transferred them from the skiff to the barge and left the tarps pulled up. We could see the live dolphins on the deck of the barge, thrashing so loudly it sounded like shotgun blasts echoing off the surrounding hills. We watched as both dolphins were gutted, fully alive, in front of our eyes. Blood gushed from the convulsing bodies onto the white boots of the dolphin hunters, splattering across the boat as their tails repeatedly slapped the deck of the boat. The cries the dolphins were emitting as their bellies were cut open, from nose to tail, pierce my ears still and makes me cringe. I will never forget that sound. Never.

November 24, 2010

I'm home in Bellingham. I long to be back in Japan. This life here seems so pointless. One of the Cove Guardians posted on Facebook today asking if anyone else was having a difficult time adjusting to life after being at the Cove. We all responded, and we all are suffering from PTSD. Being 'normal' now is impossible. The only thing keeping me going at this point is knowing I'm going back soon. The other morning my husband's alarm woke me, and the cat wouldn't stop meowing, and the neighbor was mowing the lawn and all I could think of was how desperately I didn't want to be there. I realize that my marriage was over long before I went to Japan, but now I understand that I need to actually do something about it.

December 1, 2010

I'm on the ferry to Friday Harbor, San Juan Island, Washington State, where Sea Shepherd is headquartered. I'll be spending the next two days in the office doing Skype conferences, financial advisory meetings, etc. I have a lot to learn to help me prepare to take over the role of Campaign Leader at the Cove. I'm nervous about the responsibility that will rest solely upon my shoulders, but never once have I doubted that I can handle it. I know it will be the most challenging task of my life, but I know I'm strong enough. I've always seemed to lack faith in myself and standing up for myself and my beliefs has always been difficult for me. I don't know what makes me think I'm even remotely right for this role, but I know I am. For the first time, I have absolute faith in myself, my passion, my ability and my strength.

I love my husband so deeply, and I'm so thankful for our time together. He is such a good man, but I know that our relationship has run its course. We're not right for each other anymore. He was everything I needed all those years ago when we first met. I wouldn't be who I am if he hadn't come into my life and loved me. But how do you walk away from someone you love so much? How do you do what you know is right when it hurts so severely? All those long months of marriage counseling; they seem now like just a waste of money. We would sit there, in front of a stranger, and I would cry uncontrollably and tell him how lonely I am, that I want to make things better, and he would stare at the floor, bouncing his knee up and down, and tell me he didn't understand why I was so "worked up"; that our marriage was "fine". Clearly, it's not fine and it breaks my heart to leave, but I simply have no strength left to keep trying. We've been together since 2004, and I'm exhausted. I want more out of a relationship than what he can offer me. His idea of showing love is through spending money on me. I don't want to be showered with expensive gifts or any gifts at all. I don't want or need material possessions. I don't want that brand new Subaru he bought in the hopes of making me happy. I want love – hugs, kisses, conversation, support, adventure, laughter and memories. I don't want gift certificates for day spas. But that's who he is; it's how his mother approaches love as well, and I have no right to fault him for that. We show love differently, and that's okay. But he deserves a woman who will appreciate the love-as-money thing, and I need a man who will show his love for me via roaming the world at my side and actually talking to me. I know that my life is waiting for me, out there, waiting for me to come to live it, the way I want to. I'm terrified; I feel as if I'm about to jump off a cliff, but I'm positive that my parachute will open at some point on the way down. Hopefully I'm not wrong about that...

December 9, 2010

Back in Japan. Emotions ran high today as we said tear-filled goodbyes to several Cove Guardians. Together, we are soldiers on a battlefield and the bonding that happens here is something I've never experienced before. All the Cove Guardians come together as strangers, passionate about the same cause and we end our time together as family, bonded beyond belief. Saying goodbye was difficult for everyone, but saying goodbye to the Cove itself is something that can never be described. I'm dreading the day I leave this place for good.

December 10, 2010

No matter how many times I bear witness to a slaughter, I am always taken aback by the horror of it all. Each kill brings up so many traumas from my past that I thought I had dealt with long ago. Witnessing mass murder is something I never dreamed I would experience, but here I am, in the thick of it. And though it may sound sick, there's no place I'd rather be. Some days I want to scream, some days I want to cry and some days I want to lash out and break anything I can get my hands on. Each one of us is experiencing the same emotions and although we may not have the same feeling at the same time, it's such a reassuring comfort to know that we have each other.

December 13, 2010

As I sit writing this, it's pouring down rain outside my hotel window in Kii-Katsuura and I am reminded of home; the rainy Pacific Northwest. As I sink deeper into the world of Sea Shepherd, I become more and more aware of the corruptness of this organization. We don't have enough Cove Guardians because no one wants to be associated with the childish hostility that this group condones and even encourages. They encourage hatred of anyone who's different, anyone who's not 'with us'. As Campaign Leader, I'm continuously receiving emails from Paul and Scott instructing me to shun this person, to kick that person out of the organization, to not stand next to so and so at the Cove. It's exhausting, and I feel like I'm constantly walking on egg shells. The drama. They're not happy unless they hate someone. But I'm also grateful to be where I am. I went from watching Whale Wars on TV and desperately wanting to be a part of this, straight to being a Campaign Leader in a foreign country. People around the world know who I am, and I feel like I truly am making a difference. I encourage diplomacy and kindness toward the fishermen of Taiji; I inform prospective Cove Guardians via email that once they arrive in Japan, hatred and anger will not be tolerated at the Cove. And I do all this on my own, with no support of diplomacy from Sea Shepherd. I made an executive decision when I took over as Campaign Leader that I would not condone hatred, racism and violence. So far, Paul hasn't told me to change my ways, and if he does, fuck him. Scott still continuously encourages me to use the word "molesters" to describe the fishermen, but I refuse to. When I sent in one of my first daily blogs for the SSCS website, they changed it before publication and added that word. I sent an email to headquarters telling them to change it back, to not change my words again, and to never assume that simply because I'm a part of SSCS that I'm okay with using that word. I'm becoming embarrassed by Sea Shepherd, but I also feel like the notoriety they provide me with can be used to make a positive difference. Does that make me a dick who's using SSCS for my own benefit??

December 15, 2010

Witnessing death, either on a large scale or a single instance, is something that will forever change who you are. Becoming numb and disconnected is a survival instinct that your body simply must resort to. We all handle tragedy differently and some of us are more accustomed to tragedy than others. I fall into the category of being accustomed to tragedy. However, my life has in no way hardened me to the horrors of genocide. No matter how many times I see it with my own eyes, the sight of terrified dolphins being brutally murdered is something that will haunt me forever. The screaming of dolphins, echoing off the steep cliffs of the Cove, are present in my dreams at night and make my stomach churn with guilt when I awake with a start and realize that I couldn't save them from death. But it's the sound of the banger boats that's the worst – the sound of the dolphin hunters banging with a hammer on a long metal pole held into the sea from the side of their boats, driving the dolphins into a net of sound that painfully confuses their natural echolocation. As Ric O'Barry, an internationally known marine conservationist says – "that sound never goes away, once you hear it". He was hauntingly accurate when he made that statement.

Today was a day that simply broke me. A pod of roughly 20 striped dolphins was driven into the Cove. Overcome with fear, they headed in three different directions, separating the original pod of possibly 50 dolphins. Two of the separated groups were fortunate enough to escape. One was not so lucky. The group that was driven into the Cove included at least two calves. The mother of one of the calves was in the group that escaped. More than likely she will stay in the area, searching for her baby, only to be caught by the hunters tomorrow.

Another mother, trapped in the Cove, watched as her infant struggled, tangled in a fishing net. She watched as a skiff approached her offspring, roughly pulled it from the net, tied a rope around its tail and dragged it upon the beach to its death.

December 16, 2010

I will always remember the first time I laid eyes on the Cove. Like the majority of people serving as Cove Guardians, I had seen the Academy Award winning documentary, The Cove, and was horrified beyond words. What happens in this little slice of sea is unimaginable. When the opportunity arose for me to travel to Japan, I was terrified. Coming here involved giving up my career during a time when jobs are few and far between and a decent paying job is out of the question in the failing American economy. But this was my dream, my passion, my soul's desire; so, I turned in my notice and came to Japan to serve as a Cove Guardian. My first glimpse of the Cove was awe-inspiring. It's a very surreal feeling to see something on TV and then have it before your very eyes. This area of Japan is an impressive landscape that can't be appreciated until you're actually here. Yet after my time here and seeing what happens in that finger of water along the rugged coastline, I see no more beauty at the Cove. I gaze out across the water and see suffering, pain, death and more blood than I ever thought possible.

December 18, 2010

Today was a day that has challenged me as a photographer, as a writer and as a human being. I am sitting here now, fumbling with my words, trying to find an appropriate way to explain what happened at the Cove today. The fact is, there simply aren't words to describe the callousness of the actions that took place.

A pod of roughly 20 striped dolphins was driven into the Cove; perhaps they were the remaining dolphins from the pod that was slaughtered a few days ago. Among them was a tiny baby; the smallest any of us had ever seen. Judging by its size, we estimated it to be less than a month old. Panic was ruling this baby's actions and it was repeatedly jumping completely out of the water. To pretend that I understand the fear it was feeling would be an insult to this precious little creature.

Behind my sunglasses, tears filled my eyes and it took everything I had to continue photographing. I knew when I came here that as a photographer, this would be the most challenging subject I've ever taken on. But I also knew that as a photographer, my work could potentially make a difference in the lives of these dolphins. Now, as a writer, I am trying to convey the feelings I was experiencing as I watched this innocent little thing die. I fear that I am simply not doing its memory justice, so I'll stop trying.

December 20, 2010

The days in Japan blend together. One day feels like a week. One week feels like a month. I'm not even really sure what day it is. All I know for certain lately is if the day I am currently living was a slaughter day or not. And today was a slaughter day. I'm so exhausted from constantly seeing death.

December 21, 2010

The important thing to remember, in my humble opinion, is that with humanity comes the right to believe what we wish. Human beings will never see eye to eye on all topics and forcing your opinion or beliefs upon another will in no way produce a favorable result for either party involved. A perfect example is the friction between the Cove Guardians and the dolphin hunters. It's an interesting relationship between the two groups and I wonder what will come of it in the long run. A few days ago, I approached one of the fishermen while he stood at the Cove, on his day off it seemed, watching his co-workers drive dolphins. I had a translator with me and I had something very specific I wanted to say to this man; an apology, from me to him, on behalf of former Cove Guardians who had shamefully taunted him. When I tried to get his attention, he simply turned his back on me and would not acknowledge me. I was speaking Japanese to him and still I was hitting a brick wall. I spoke what Japanese I could, and then told the translator what I wished to say and asked him to say it to this man's back, knowing that he would at least hear the words. I know that the words reached not only his ears, but also his heart, because today when we saw him, he made eye contact with me and slightly bowed, which is something that has never happened before. Progress comes when respect is present, and I've been ashamed to witness the high number of Sea Shepherd Cove Guardians who have absolutely no respect for anything, let alone these men who work at the Cove. There have been so many times when I've felt ashamed to be associated with this group, and it seems that the 'higher-ups' are encouraging this disgusting display of disdain; of childish taunting of the dolphin hunters. The Campaign Leader before me would encourage the Cove Guardians to surround a single fisherman and say the most horrid things to them, while filming it all, and then put it on YouTube as a mark of pride. Comments such as them deserving the bomb we dropped on them are a regular occurrence and I find it absolutely infuriating and fucking disgusting that men like him are allowed to be in charge. I question daily my involvement with Sea Shepherd, but it's too late now. I've given up everything for them. Where else am I going to go?? And I am thankful to be where I am, doing what I am. Sea Shepherd has provided me with the opportunity to live my passion, and now that I'm the Campaign Leader I have the authority to change the embarrassingly childish behavior that was so prevalent under the previous Campaign Leader.

December 22, 2010

Being a Cove Guardian is exhausting work. The emotional drain takes more of a toll than any physical work I've ever experienced. We wake up early every single day, with no hope of a day to sleep in. We stand for hours, scanning the horizon with binoculars, and it's so cold right now, waiting for the banger boats to appear. On the no-kill days, we try to do some sightseeing but usually end up in the hotel lobby on our computers. And of course, on kill days, we witness tragedy. And then we end up in the hotel lobby on our computers.

But this is also the most rewarding work I've ever done and being here is an incredible feeling. I am willing to sacrifice sleep and suffer some emotional trauma if it will help save just one single dolphin. This is my passion and I feel blessed to be living this life.

I realize that some people might have a negative opinion about Japan in general. People hear that the Japanese are killing dolphins and of course are outraged, as well they should be. But Japan is my home for the next three months and I am continually impressed with the friendliness of the people, the cleanliness of the towns, the majestic beauty of the landscape and let's not forget the absolutely amazing food. I come from a nation that is disliked by many other countries and there are numerous actions done by America's leaders that I don't agree with. There are actions taken by groups of people that I don't agree with. But I would hope that I personally would not be judged because of those things. The majority of the general public in Japan isn't even aware that this is happening and it's wrong to judge them based on something they know nothing of. The racism that seems to run rampant within SSCS and its volunteers is astounding and shocking and disgusting.

December 23, 2010

Tonight, as we walked to the gym, a Japanese guy about our age pulled his car over and asked us if we were the Cove Guardians. As members of Sea Shepherd, we're taught to be suspicious of everyone. I feel it's nearly demanded of us. As a friendly person, suspicion is something that doesn't come naturally to me, but I'm simply a pawn in the Sea Shepherd shit show, so I do what I'm told. This man started talking so quickly (in Japanese, of course) and with such happy emotion that it was impossible for us to follow what he was saying, but it was obvious that he was ecstatic to have had a "Cove Guardian sighting". He was motioning with his hands that he is very much against the dolphin slaughter and kept pointing to us and saying things like "great" and "thank you". We received many bows of gratitude and an endless supply of smiles - a very universal language.

The support of the local citizens is mind blowing at times and it's exactly what this campaign needs to completely shut down the dolphin hunting industry. People are often upset that we don't rent boats and try to drive dolphins away from the banger boats or hop into our wetsuits and attempt to cut nets. Instant gratification is not the purpose of our presence and even if we wanted to cut nets and sink boats, it's nearly impossible to do so without then being a not-so-honored guest of a lovely Japanese prison. These dolphins don't need us to break the law, get deported and be banned from the country; they need us to approach this situation with a clear mind and diplomacy to find a way to stop it.

December 25, 2010

If someone had told me a few months ago that I would be celebrating Christmas in Japan, I would have thought them insane. But here I am, enjoying one of the best Christmases of my life with my new friends, most of who are from countries very different than my own. Life brought each and every one of us here to be in this place, in this moment and it's so amazing to me that I am a part of it.

In the wee hours of the morning one of the women who works the front desk of our hotel was down in the lobby busily decorating a Christmas tree. When we came down that morning, it was decorated and lit up, displayed there to make us feel more at home. Christmas isn't a holiday that's widely celebrated in Japan and the fact that this wonderful woman went to great lengths to put up a tree and decorate it in the early morning hours proves just how accommodating the Japanese people are. She had even gone so far as to have her son, who lives in New York City, mail her Christmas ornaments. I was so moved by her selfless act of generosity and genuine concern for us that I wanted to throw my arms around her and cry.

Tonight, on Christmas night, we sat in the hotel lobby swapping stories, sharing laughter, passing chocolate around and watching episodes of Whale Wars. The atmosphere was one of contentment and peace. And while the fear of what tomorrow will bring is always in the back of our minds, tonight we were happy for the moment to simply...be.

December 26, 2010

Throughout my childhood, I wanted nothing more than to be a dolphin trainer. Even as a very young child, I was so in love with these creatures that it was nearly too much for my little heart and soul to handle. When I was eight, my mom took me and my brother and sister to Marine Land in San Diego and as we watched the orcas and dolphins perform, I just knew that I was destined to someday be a trainer. However, as is the norm with life, as I got older my fairytale shattered and I started to understand the truth about captivity and about how inhumanely horrible it is. My views on wildlife began to change and I discovered the amazing world of conservation and activism. And now I find myself here, in Japan, protesting a dolphin slaughter and actively using my passion for writing to help make a difference. Life is pretty dang crazy, yo.

December 27, 2010

The other night, we ran into a group of teenage girls that were so excited to see us and were speaking what little English they knew to us. It's amazing to me, living in a country where we understand hardly any of the language, how it's possible to carry on a conversation despite the language barrier. Humans are humans and despite the differences in culture, language, etc. we are all basically the same.

What we witness here is beyond explanation; we see things that most people will never experience; things most people could never even imagine. Each and every one of us came to Taiji knowing full well that we would see dolphins die. I can't tell you how many people back home said to me that they simply would not be able to handle watching that happen. Yet, here we are, watching it happen because all of us are passionate enough about saving these dolphins that we're willing to bear witness to horrible acts of inhumanity. There are no words for what this does to our mental state and we have to consciously be aware of controlling our anger, our frustration, our pain and our sadness. And it all falls to me to keep everyone in line as well. It's crazy being "in charge"; being the one over here on foreign soil that's responsible for all the Cove Guardians. It's a big super stressful burden. And the world either loves me or hates me because I'm the face and voice for SSCS on this campaign. Being hated is something entirely new for me and it hurts my heart. I've always been a kind, friendly person because I've never wanted someone to feel that unwanted feeling that I've experienced for a good portion of my life. But Sea Shepherd encourages me to act unfriendly, to act with suspicion and portray arrogance. It's something I'm struggling to do, and I feel constantly aware of how people currently perceive me. I feel like a fucking bitch, something I've never really been. Several times I've been told that I'm 'scary' or 'intimidating' and that makes me feel so terrible that people feel that way about me. But the stress of being under the thumb of Sea Shepherd is crushing; I'm very much aware of the way being involved with this group is altering my personality. It's a very dirty feeling, but I'm not sure what to do about it at this point. Being with Sea Shepherd means being this way, and before I realized that about them, I chose to be a part of it all. I drank their damn Kool-Aide and now I don't know how to get out. I feel like a different person...a person I don't like very much.

December 30, 2010

Yesterday, we filmed what we thought to be an empty pool at Dolphin Base, where they train the dolphins to perform, with water so still that it was collecting algae. When we reviewed the footage back at the hotel, we were shocked to learn that there was a dolphin in the tank. More footage was taken and it's now clear that this dolphin is floating in a dirty tank, all alone. There's no pump in the pool so the water is near stagnant, with green algae ringing the waterline.

Andy stood on Tim's shoulders, so they could film over the fence. When this lone little dolphin noticed the camera being hoisted over the top of the fence, he started to move around and at one point even tried to encourage the camera to play with the yellow buoy it was holding in its mouth.

Initially, I didn't think anything could be more sickeningly heartbreaking then the sight of a depressed dolphin floating on the surface, holding a buoy like a child would a teddy bear. When the dolphin tried to interact with the camera and was encouraging playfulness with the buoy, I stood corrected. He was desperate for attention and interaction and it crushed my heart beyond belief. I nearly couldn't comprehend the tragedy of it all. I feel so fortunate to have made such amazing friends here at the Cove. It's unbelievable how deeply we've all bonded. Sometimes, after a bad slaughter day, we'll all meet up in my hotel room (because I'm campaign mom!) and I'll make everyone grilled cheese sandwiches with the most amazing Japanese bread and Kewpie mayonnaise and then we'll all snuggle and watch a movie. We fit six of us on my tiny twin bed one time to watch a movie! But that human contact when we're all suffering so deeply is vital, and I'm so grateful to have people to comfort me.

December 31, 2010

Time is something that is more than likely running out for the dolphin we discovered at Dolphin Base. When we, along with the team from Ric O'Barry's Dolphin Project, took footage of the dolphin, we had no idea that it would spread around the world like wildfire. This depressed little dolphin, with the ever-present buoy in its mouth, has now been named Misty and a Facebook page has been created by supporters called "Save Misty the Dolphin". It's crazy. I didn't realize how this would take off. But everything here is crazy. And the fishermen have been on an extended Christmas break so there haven't been any drives happening. I guess people need something to focus on.

We visited Misty again today and found him (yes, we were told by Misty's vet that it's a boy, but he wouldn't tell us his name, so Misty it is...) to be floating in the same spot as yesterday, clutching its yellow buoy. The tank is estimated to be around eight feet deep, which is about the length of the dolphin, and green algae is rapidly overtaking the water.

January 4, 2011

Last night held some activity. Misty was moved out of his filthy algae-ridden tank and placed in a tank with about five other dolphins.

I finally got Misty's vet to agree to an interview, which I recorded with my iPhone without his knowledge (I'm a dick). He told me that Misty was scheduled to be moved within the next few days. We had a continuous watch at Dolphin Base and were able to be on location when they started moving Misty. The Dolphin Base staff waited until late in the evening to execute the move and Misty was transported from one tank to the other in the dark. We were all spread around filming the move from different locations. Andy was on the hillside; Nicole and I were huddled together against the bitter cold at the top of a fire escape at the neighboring hotel. The cops found us, though, and we took off running with the cops chasing us. Talk about adrenaline. All I could hear was our breathing as we ran. All I could see in the pitch black was the bounce of the cop's flashlight behind us. I couldn't see in front of me, but I just kept running.

When I introduced Misty to the world five days ago people started calling and emailing Dolphin Base, questioning the treatment of this dolphin, and it made a difference. It made such a large impact that the staff at Dolphin Base went as far as to mention to me the amount of calls and emails they were receiving and asked me to tell the world to please stop calling. It's bizarre to me that the world listens to me; that I'm now someone of importance that somehow holds sway over others. The fact that the vet at Dolphin Base has asked me to address the world, knowing that they will listen, is something I still can't quite get used to. But I want to use this new-found power for good, and it seems that each day I'm a part of Sea Shepherd brings something bad.

It feels like I've been here a year. My husband and I have only talked once. We've even stopped emailing. I know we're done, and he knows we're done and I feel guilty for not being more upset about that. I think it's this place, though. I don't have time to be lonely or homesick or think about my marriage. On the one hand, that's sad, but on the other hand, I'm thankful. I simply could not handle more heartbreak right now.

January 5, 2011

We visited Misty again today after his big move to a new tank and were so happy to see that he seems to be doing better. They let him keep his yellow buoy and today he was tossing it in the air, trying to entice the dolphins in the next tank to play.

I find myself questioning nearly every day the ethics of Sea Shepherd. The more involved I become, the more I'm exposed to private emails and the inner workings of the organization, the more I see how gross and ethically barren this group is.

January 14, 2011

Blood was spilled in the Cove again today. Being an activist is challenging to a degree of no comparison. Choosing to live the lifestyle of an activist has cost me dearly in certain aspects of my life. I've been alienated from family members, given up my career, walked away from my marriage and put everything on the line to stand up for what I believe in. But when you're passionate about something, you have to give it your all. If you don't live for something, you'll die for nothing and I've witnessed firsthand, and not just here in Taiji, that everything can be torn from you in an instant and that life can cease in a heartbeat. Life is too precious and too short to live a life you're not in love with.

January 16, 2011

Seeing death every day in Taiji has forced me to prioritize my life and decide which direction I want to take, which path I want to walk and what type of person I want to be. There is no going back to "normal" life after spending time at the Cove. Things that plagued my mind two months ago now seem so incredibly petty and insignificant. I know for a fact that once my time in Taiji is up and I head home to Seattle, my life will not be the same. As difficult as it's been, I'm incredibly grateful for this experience and I know that the Cove is a place that will remain with me for the rest of my days.

January 18, 2011

When I was younger and dreamed of saving dolphins, I didn't imagine that I would be doing it in a foreign country and trying to communicate with prideful men that despise me for impeding their livelihood. Nor did I imagine that I would witness dolphins throwing themselves against jagged rocks while wrapped in the throes of disorienting fear. Life, man...I tell you what.

Today about 40 striped dolphins were driven into the Cove and, consumed by terror to the point of leaping out of the water and onto the rocks, they became bloody and disabled. The question remains as to if this is a conscious act of desperation on the dolphin's part or if they are so overcome with fear that they're unaware of what they're doing. Perhaps,

178

being as how it's a proven fact that dolphins are just as intelligent as humans (we all know at least one human that definitely isn't smarter than a dolphin), this is an instinct that kicks in when they know they're facing their own mortality. I always try to put myself in the dolphin's shoes, so to speak, and think about what I would do if I found myself knocking on deaths door. If I were moments away from being murdered, would I attempt suicide as well? Death by your own hand is better than a degrading and humiliating exit from life at the hand of a being that feels no respect for your life, nor the loss of that life. I've experienced the murder of a loved one and it is a horror of unimaginable proportions.

For these dolphins to be present, to witness the barbaric destruction of their families, to swim in the blood of their kin, is something that I can't even pretend to understand. I feel so pathetically helpless, so disgustingly powerless while this is happening before my eyes. I feel ridiculous for worrying about the petty things in life. This world is full of horror; but it is also full of good and there are so many amazing people out there who care so deeply and passionately about things that touch the soul.

January 20, 2011

I'm baffled as to how a human being can severe a dolphin's spinal cord, club a baby seal or skin a cat alive for its fur. Cruelty is a concept that I don't understand, even when it's cruelty in the instance of the 'mean girl' who torments others in the school halls. Humans are the cruelest of all species; not only to creatures that we feel to be beneath us, but to each other as well. We call our race superior because of things we've accomplished and granted, we have accomplished an impressive amount, but look at what we've destroyed in the process. Look at what we continue to knowingly destroy for the sake of progress. We're mutilating this planet and even though we realize this fact, we still won't stop. And why do those of us who care get so much shit for caring? I've encountered people that enjoy making fun of me for caring about the planet and for some, it seems, not recycling and not caring about animal welfare is almost a matter of pride for them. There's one dude that I worked with at Grizzly that was such a fucking douche about the whole animal rights thing. It was like jokingly making fun of me was the only way he knew how to have a conversation with me. What a dick head.

I can't even begin to explain what I'm feeling about my marriage right now. All I know is that I simply cannot go home to him, to a lonely and loveless marriage. I feel all these emotions so deeply and I feel the need to write, like I always do when I'm dealing with strong emotions, but what can I say? What can I write that I haven't already? I'm just too tired...

February 2, 2011

Although my head is fucked from this experience in Japan, I know it's changed me for the better. I'm stronger, more confident and capable. I simply cannot go home to a relationship where I am so desperately lonely. And how many times have I voiced my loneliness to him? It seems like a million, in a million different ways. He's not a talker; that's just the way he is. Who am I to change that about him? Each day here, I feel like I'm going to explode, and I cry every time I'm alone. I'm so damn tired. My heart and my mind have gone numb. So often these days Nicole and I will just hold each other and cry. The other night we huddled onto my little bed with Andy and the three of us listened to really sad music and stared at the ceiling. It feels as if we floated in the oblivion, together yet alone, for years.

February 3, 2011

Life is something I don't understand. My mom skyped me early this morning before I left for the Cove to tell me that Jesse

Maurer had been killed in a car accident in my hometown. Jesse. My dear friend from so long ago. Dead. After the call, I opened my hotel door, Andy and Nicole had their doors open as well, and I just started crying in the hall. They both rushed out and encircled me in their loving arms. Jesse is dead, and now I'm going to the Cove to watch dolphins being senselessly and ruthlessly slaughtered. I am so fucking over this place.

February 13, 2011

I'm so depressed these days, it's starting to scare me. Most of the Cove Guardians live in Australia; they'll have each other when our time here ends. I'll have no one. There's no way my husband is going to understand what I'll be going through when I get home. None of my friends in Bellingham will understand. And I don't want to talk to them anyway. How can I ever comprehensively describe to someone what it's like to be in Taiji? You can't. You just can't. There's no possible way. I don't know what will happen when I get home, but I have a feeling my world is about to go up in flames. And I'm the one lighting the match. I am so sad, I feel like I'm drowning.

February 15, 2011

Two weeks exactly. At this time in two weeks, I'll be on a plane headed home to Seattle. It's so bizarre to think that this won't be my life anymore. But I'm so ready to not be here. I have no idea what will happen when I get home. Will I fall back into the mundane security of life in the suburbs? Or will I stand by my convictions and do what I want with my life? I love my husband, so deeply, but I simply cannot live his life any longer. Life is so short and so precious and can be over in an instant. I need to live my own life, exactly the way I want to live it. Roaming the world. Doing meaningful work that sets my heart on fire. Loving and being loved by a man who somehow just simply...gets me. My husband definitely does not get me. Like at all. He thinks I'm ridiculous for having so much passion, for wanting to see every little nook and cranny of this beautiful world we live in. He tells me all the time that I need to "calm down" when I'm happy and expressing joy. Why the fuck would you tell someone to calm down when they're happy? He told me that at a concert once. We had gone up to Stanley Park in Vancouver to see Metric. I got him tickets for his birthday. They were amazing, but he just sat there on the blanket with no emotion on his face. I got up and was dancing. When I came back to the blanket he told me that I needed to "calm down". I told him it was okay for him to smile in public and then disappeared into the crowd. Calm down? Fuck off.

February 17, 2011

I'm sitting on my bed in my little hotel room in Katsuura, Japan listening to the rain fall down outside my open window. I leave this place in just over a week. It's going by so quickly, yet so slowly. I don't want to leave, but I'm ready to be gone. I don't want to go home. I don't want to deal with my problems. I just want to run off somewhere and be alone. I am so depressed I can hardly function. It's nighttime right now, and it's raining. I'm listening to sad music. What will it be like when I go home? I'll have no one. I can't count on my husband for emotional support.

February 19, 2011

It's 10:14pm. We just had an earthquake. We were going to bed and the entire hotel began shaking. We all ran out into the hall and just looked at each other, wide-eyed, while the building shook for quite a long time (unbeknownst to us at the time, the earthquakes we were feeling were precursors to the earthquake and tsunami that hit on March 11, 2011).

I had such a wonderful conversation with Nicole tonight. We sat on my bed listening to music and talking about everything. I can't believe I only have nine days left with her. She's been my lifeline all these months in Japan. Part of my soul will go back to Australia with her, and I already feel the empty space in my heart.

Today was such a brutal slaughter. The striped dolphins are always the worst. They throw themselves onto the rocks, which shreds their skin into bloody ribbons. It's unbearable to watch.

February 20, 2011

It terrifies me that I don't miss my husband after being away from him for so many months. It terrifies me that I so desperately don't want to go home to him. That makes me feel like the worst person in the world; the worst wife in the world. I love him, but I can't sacrifice myself to be with him any longer. He deserves someone who will love him for who he is, someone who wants to live the same life he does, someone he can shower with gifts as replacements for affection. That person isn't me. And I deserve someone who will love me exactly the way I am; someone who won't want or try to change me. I can't live that materialistic life any longer. He finally is making the money he wants and who am I to keep him from spending it the way he wants? He shouldn't be forced into my frugal lifestyle when it's his money. He wants someone who won't view it as his money, but our money, and I can't do that. I can't live off someone else. He deserves someone different than me.

February 22, 2011

I never thought I would be spending my 30th birthday in Japan, let alone spending it watching dolphins die on a regular basis; but I suppose we never truly know what life has planned for us, because here I am in Japan, on my 30th birthday, watching dolphins die on a regular basis. The staff at the hotel where we live gave me flowers; the Steve Irwin crew sent me a nautical *chart that they all signed. I was given presents by the Cove Guardians and skyped with friends in Australia. What a day!*

February 26, 2011

The dolphin slaughter season ended today. And while I'm happy, I simply have nothing left in me to give. My head hurts. My heart hurts. My soul feels shattered. I'm so, so tired.

February 27, 2011

Tomorrow is our last full day in Japan. I don't know if I feel sad or happy about leaving. The group of Cove Guardians that is here right now are such douche bags. All they do is sit in the lobby of the hotel at night and get drunk. Drinking is not what this campaign is about, and if someone can't handle this place without getting shitty drunk, they're in the wrong fucking place. My respect for Sea Shepherd has pretty much tanked during my time here. But again, I have nowhere else to go. I gave up everything to join this organization. I feel like I have no choice now except to continue to drink their Kool-aid and ignore the fact that Sea Shepherd is akin to a cult. I chose this, I wanted this, and now it's too late. I'm stuck in it.

March 1, 2011

Again, I find myself on an airplane. I feel like I've spent half my life in the air, and I can't believe that I just spent the past four months living in Asia. I don't want to go home, but that's where I'm heading now. And the fact that I don't want to go home makes me feel so guilty. I should miss my husband and our life together because it's a good life and he's a good husband. It's the life that so many people dream of. But yet, here I sit, 30,000 feet above who-knows-what, crying in the darkness of the plane. It's not right to feel this way.

March 4, 2011

I'll never forget the day that I arrived home from Japan. I landed in SeaTac, broken beyond repair it seemed. My husband collected me from the airport and we drove the two hours home to Bellingham in silence. I cried silently, the tears burning my face, and watched the rain streak across the passenger window. He didn't say a word to me, nor I to him. What was there to say? I was haunted by the dolphin slaughter I had witnessed. I walked through the front door of our house, greeted by my pets, and went straight to my hiding place under the blankets of a bed I hadn't slept in for four months. In the days that followed, I was swallowed whole by my sadness. I was left alone, my husband at work, to struggle with the weight of my destroyed life.

March 5, 2011

It's official – I'm getting a divorce. My husband told me today (in an email) that I need to decide if I want to stay or go. The fact that he would be okay if I stayed even though I've been telling him for years that I'm unhappy is a perfect indicator of how complacent he is. I told him that I can't live like this any longer. I clearly didn't make the decision he wanted me to because now he talks to me even less than he did before and being in the house together is awkward. But I'm getting my things packed. This depression and PTSD is kicking my ass. I haven't eaten for nearly the whole week I've been home. I can't function. I space off while I'm driving and then can't remember which side of the road I'm meant to be driving on. I'm so damn tired and am having such trouble carrying on a conversation. I'm still not dreaming at night. I stopped dreaming in Japan. I thought the nightmares that have plagued me my entire life would come back once I was home, but they haven't, and not dreaming seems to make me so much more tired than the actual nightmares.

Later in the day…

I've packed my few belongings, leaving the dishes in the kitchen cupboard, the towels in the hall closet, and walked out. Numb, I drove to my parent's house in Southern Oregon and again retreated to the safety under the blankets. My life feels over. My marriage is definitely over. As I stood in the open doorway of the home I shared with my husband, my packed bags in the car and the dog whining at my feet, I asked my husband to say something, anything, begging him, without saying the words, to ask me to stay. He sat on the couch playing his video games, bouncing his knee up and down, and the words he chose solidified all my pain. "Text me when you get to your mom's house". That was it; we were both giving up. And it was such a relief.

At my parent's house, I am suffocating. The PTSD I'm experiencing has sucked the very life out of me. Gone is my smile, my laughter, my ability to have a conversation. The tears well up and run over with no warning and the exhaustion leaves me feeling hollow. It was my mother who came to my rescue. She sent me to a therapist, got me on anti-depressants and enrolled me in a SCUBA certification class. She is such a good mom. What would I do without her? But it was the offer from Sea Shepherd to join the crew of the Steve Irwin that truly saved my life.

May 10, 2011

I'm officially the proud owner of a plane ticket to France. In less than a week I'll be flying to France to live and crew aboard the M/Y Steve Irwin in the Mediterranean. I am beyond ready for better days; to move past the sickness inside my head that was caused by the dolphin slaughter.

Two months after I left Japan, I'm boarding a flight from Medford, Oregon to join the ship in Cannes, France. I am in motion once again, and at 30,000 feet, with the beauty of the world stretched out below me, I'm finally beginning to feel alive again. There's no time to feel sorry for myself because of the tragedies I've seen and experienced - I have airports to navigate, luggage to drag behind me and endless possibilities to imagine. I have a ship waiting for me in the South of France. A ship full of people just like me...

Aboard the M/Y Steve Irwin:

May 18, 2011

Medford, OR to Denver, CO to Washington DC to Zurich, Switzerland to Nice, France. Then a bus from Nice to Cannes. I'm joining the Steve Irwin. After years of watching Whale Wars on TV, I'm actually joining the Steve. And although I gave up my entire world to be here, it has all been worth it. I would make the same decisions again in an instant. You only remember one life at a time...

June 4, 2011

I haven't had any time to write since I've been aboard the Steve. There's constantly people around. But I adore this life so far. I feel like this is where I was born to be. I know I need to be writing while I'm here, but just like in Taiji, my words can never accurately describe all that's happening, or all I'm feeling. I've been on the ship for over two weeks now and it feels like a lifetime, but in such a good and beautiful way. I feel like this is my home, like this is where I belong. We've seen dolphins off the bow twice so far and seeing them in the wild, away from the Cove, thriving and healthy in the deep blue, overwhelmed my heart and brought tears to my eyes. The Mediterranean sun is blazing, and the ship work is brutally physical. My soul finally feels as if it's healing – healing from all the shit in my past, from the trauma of watching dolphins die at the Cove, from leaving my husband. Not having internet, nor any connection to the outside world, is such a blessing right now. I'm simply here, soaking in every gorgeous minute of this life.

June 5, 2011

Last night I gave a presentation to my crewmates about Taiji. They were so attentive and all of them have told me since my first day on the ship that they followed the campaign in Japan, that they read my daily updates on the Sea Shepherd website out loud every night in the crew mess, that they are proud of me. After my slideshow, there were dolphins off the bow again so we all raced up there and leaned way over to marvel at them, feeling the salty spray dust our faces. It was beautiful. I love being out in the middle of the ocean, with no land in sight, no contact with anyone except these lovely people. I don't miss anyone. This is where I want to be, this is what I want to be doing. So many people have been emailing and warning me to not get too involved with Sea Shepherd. I understand their concern, and I see it myself, but it's too late now. I'm here and I'm in love with this ship. But I feel as if I'm constantly walking a tightrope; like at any moment, I could step wrong and everything will be ruined.

June 7, 2011

I went out in the Delta (inflatable boat) today and we put divers in the water to train for cutting tuna nets. We were testing different recall methods to call the divers back to the Delta. One method was putting a long metal pole into the water and banging on it with a hammer, exactly how the fishermen in Taiji drive the dolphins into the Cove. When I heard that sound, I was instantly taken back to Taiji, to hearing that horrid sound of clanking metal. The shock of that sound stung my eyes with tears and made me sick to my stomach. Sometimes, just driving down the road, passing construction, I hear that sound, and it whips me back to the Cove, to watching dolphins die. I still feel so hollow when I remember my experiences there. I wonder if that will ever go away.

June 10, 2011

We're docked in Syracuse, Italy on the Isle of Sicily. It's one of the oldest cities in the Mediterranean. Night before last I spent hours walking around the city with two of my shipmates. I never imagined I would ever see Italy, but here I am, and it's like a beautiful dream, traveling the world aboard this ship, full of people just like me. I'm seeing the world in the most romantic way possible and I feel as if eventually the glass room I'm dancing in will shatter, and I'll find myself in the Bog of Eternal Stench with Sir Ditymus and Ludo. This fairytale I'm living can't be real; it can't last forever, can it...?

June 11, 2011

Today was fucking amazing! I was woken up this morning at 5:30am by the media director of the ship opening my cabin door and telling me that I was needed on the bridge to photograph an impending action against a tuna poacher. We had encountered a group of six purse-seining vessels and the deck team was instructed to put the Delta in the water and standby. The bosun asked if I would be willing to go out in the Delta and take still shots. Of course, I agreed, even knowing that it was potentially dangerous. That's why I'm here – to actively fight for what I believe in. The Tunisian fishermen put three inflatable boats in the water when they saw us approach. It was nine vessels against our one, and they were angry. Every boat in these waters knows who we are. They know what we're here to do and they don't like it; they don't like us. They began chasing us in their inflatable boat, throwing metal chain links and mooring rings at us. We put our helmets on, riot gear donated to us by the French police, and a moment later the Animal Planet filmmaker sitting next to me was struck in the head with a 10-inch mooring ring. The small inflatable boats were trying to prop-foul us and ram us, much like we do with the Japanese whaling vessels in Antarctica, and our driver wasn't backing down. During all the intensity there was a moment of immense peace within me; everything went calm, and it was as if I were watching everything happen in slow motion on a movie screen. I remember thinking "I'm actually here. I'm actually doing this". I was taken aback by the fact that this is my life now, that I am finally actually living my life, and living it the way I have always dreamed of. It was such an all-encompassing feeling and I realize now that I can never go back to any type of mundane life after having experienced this. I could never have stayed married, working as a photographer for an industrial company and making mortgage payments. That's not what I want, and for the first time in my 30 years, I'm finally (finally!) doing exactly what I want! And despite the high level of danger that was swirling around me out there today in the middle of the ocean, surrounded by angry Tunisians, never did I feel a speck of fear. I trusted my crewmates, and I trust where I am.

After dinner tonight, we all gathered on the bow and had a jam session. Some of the deck team were playing the fiddle and ukulele and we all danced and clapped and laughed and watched the sun set over the middle of the Mediterranean. All my life, I've either lived in the past or the future. Never have I seemed content to live in the present, but sitting on that bow tonight with my crewmates, I was so blissfully happy in the here and now.

But is it fucked up that today was one of the best days I've had in my life...and today is also my husband's birthday? I can't email him because we don't have wifi way out here in the middle of the ocean. He's better off without me anyway. He deserves a woman who will love him the way he wants to be loved; a woman who's willing and happy to share the same lifestyle that he wants. That woman isn't me.

June 14, 2011

I was stung by a jelly today. We anchored off shore of an Italian island closer to Africa called Lampedusa in order to refuel the Bridget Bardot, our scout vessel who is on campaign with us. We were allowed to go into town for the afternoon, so I went ashore with Holly and we walked around town for a bit and then met up with some of the others. As we walked, we came across armed guards in front of a vast landscape of wooden rafts, piled so high they blocked out the sun when you stood before them. The Geo Magazine photographer that was traveling with us told us they were refugee rafts from Libya. I've never seen anything like it. Hundreds, thousands of rickety homemade rafts, most looking as if they were made from pallets, were heaped one upon the other, the people who occupied them either drowned during the risky sea crossing from Africa or were being detained in the island's immigrant reception center. We learned that more than 35,000 immigrants were currently on the island due to the rebellions in Libya and Tunisia. Even though I really have nothing - no home, no job, no money – seeing those rafts made me realize that I have so much. I have freedom and happiness and despite the danger involved with being a part of Sea Shepherd, I really am relatively safe. It was humbling to be faced with the desperation that those rafts portrayed.

When we arrived back to the Steve, we decided to go swimming and we all jumped over the side of the ship into the bluest and deepest waters I've ever seen. The rays of sunshine seemed to be coming from below, deep down, from some beautiful Atlantis that we were oblivious to. I swam pretty far out from the ship and there was a moment when I realized there was a vast nothingness below my dangling legs. I felt small, insignificant, and so immensely alive. And then I was stung by a jelly and I felt searing, nearly unbearable pain. I was literally paralyzed with pain and couldn't swim. I had my mask on, and I kept sinking below the surface. One of my crewmates grabbed me and dragged me back up onto the deck of the Bridget Bardot. The doctor scraped the nettles out of my arm and doused me with vinegar. My entire right arm was covered in burn-like welts, from my hand all the way up past my elbow, wrapping around my wrist twice. As my arm was being scraped with the back of a knife to get the nettles out, I simply stood there watching, but later, when I was alone with

192

James in his cabin I cried about how much it had hurt. He held me and told me that he had no idea it hurt that badly; that I had been so stoic in front of the others. The doctor gave me pain killers and Benadryl and I'm getting ready to crawl into bed so James can hold me in his arms and read to me while I fall asleep. Today was the best day.

June 16, 2011

I am so utterly and blissfully happy. I'm happy. I'm completely in love with this life that I'm living. The ship, the travel, the cause, the people. I love every moment and every aspect. We're currently anchored off the Italian island of Pantelleria, still near Africa. Today James and I walked around town and found a beach with an abandoned tile factory and chunks of tile strewn across the sand. Everywhere. Tile as far as you could see. We collected some for souvenirs. When we got back to the ship we played Frisbee on the boat deck, just the two of us, and did our laundry in five gallon buckets of fresh water. When the sun went down, James got his violin and played Celtic music on the bow. The city lights were twinkling over the water as the sky turned orange. It was amazingly surreal and peaceful and perfect and I'm in awe of my own happiness. I never want this perfect moment in life to end. But my foreboding feeling in regard to Sea Shepherd and the morals of the organization are starting to gnaw at my insides, although I'll never voice that to anyone. How can I? You don't question Sea Shepherd; we all know that. In a lot of ways, I feel as if I were tricked into joining a cult and now I'm not sure how to get out, or if I even want to.

June 17, 2011

Today after our ship work was done, James brought a blanket up to the bow and we basked in the sunshine while he read me a story about a shipwreck. We laid there until the sun set and it began to get cold. It was beyond magical. Life baffles me. Here

I am, living on a ship in the middle of the big blue, falling so unexpectedly in love with a man who reads aloud and sings to me and kisses me on the cheek in greeting.

June 20, 2011

Today was blissful. Amazing. I did ship tours all day on the dock in Barcelona and it was so great to talk with people and share my love for conservation and have them listen intently. We arrived in Spain yesterday. Barcelona is spectacular. I've never thought twice about this city, but now that I'm here, it has truly captured my heart. Tonight, after work, James and I walked around the city. It was spellbinding. I couldn't stop smiling. We walked hand in hand through cobblestone alleys and side streets while he sang aloud. My god, that man is incredible. I know I just started writing about him out of the blue, with no explanation as to who he is. We've been hanging out together for a couple weeks now. He's the ships Bosun, from Australia. He's simply incredible. Sweet and kind, but such a man. I know that whatever we have here on the ship will end when I leave next month, but after much deliberation, I've decided to simply enjoy this entire phenomenal experience and not worry about what happens next. I love fighting for my beliefs. I love traveling the world on a ship. I love spending time with James. I love everything about life in this very moment, and I intend to fully absorb it all. Japan seems so far away and it's strange to think that I only left there three months ago. I feel like a different person already. This ship is healing my soul.

June 24, 2011

Can life really be this amazing? Is it really possible that I'm this incredibly happy? I simply cannot fathom the reality that I nearly missed out on this wonderful amazingness for a life that consisted of running the rat race and enduring a lonely marriage. This new life of mine is fucking mind blowing. I'm in

Barcelona, Spain with a wonderful man and living on a ship filled with good people who share the same passion as me. Is this real?? I could never go back to the unfulfilling life I had only less than a year ago...

July 12, 2011

Lerwick, Shetland Islands, Scotland. That's where I currently am, and it is stunning. Everything I pictured Scotland to be. We arrived today, and the ship will be leaving on the 16th. Without me. It's time for me to go home. Home to a place that never really felt like my home. Home to a place I desperately don't want to be. My world has suddenly become so black. I'm leaving. Leaving the ship, leaving this life, leaving James. I love him. How could I not? But I haven't told him that. He's incredible and I've fallen so deeply in love with him, and completely on accident. My time on this ship was supposed to be about taking time away from men, healing from my divorce. Although my husband and I were finished long ago, and I've already dealt with those feelings, I still wanted to be alone; to be with me. I was blindsided by James and my instant feelings for him. But now it's time to part ways and I feel a heaviness crushing my airways. For the first time in my life, I'm living exactly the way I want, exactly the life I want, and now it's ending. But I will forever cherish this time. I will forever hold in my heart the moment, just a few days ago, when James walked into the crew mess while I was sweeping the floor, grabbed me and started dancing with me in front of everyone. There was no music, but we didn't need any. We were dancing and laughing and looking into each other's eyes like no one else in the world existed. Forever, forever will I cherish this time in my life. Yet I also feel it's time to move on; it's time to figure my life out, to clean up the mess I've been running from back home. It's time to break free from the dictatorship that is Sea Shepherd.

July 14, 2011

I've always dreamed of seeing Scotland, but never did I imagine that I would be sitting in an outdoor coffee shop in the Lerwick harbor on the Shetland Islands. But here I am, doing exactly that; sipping my caramel latte in the sunshine. In this moment, I am happy. James and I had the day off together yesterday and it was the most perfect day. A perfect conclusion to the magic. We were away from the ship for nearly ten hours. We rode bikes all over this island. We started by sitting in a little outdoor café where we ran into the local harbor guys who helped us dock the ship. We then rode to the cemetery at the southern tip of the island. We came back into town for lunch, which we took to a little beach next to the Queen's Hotel. James took a nap in the sand while I searched for sea glass. Then we rode around the coast of the island. We went up a road to the top of the island and came to a dead end at a little farm. There were cows and sheep and the greenest pastures overlooking the sea. We lay down in the grass and took a nap in each other's arms, the warm sunshine blanketing our salt-covered skin. We must have been up there for hours. We fed grass to the horses and watched the seals in the bay. The other night we watched the movie Ondine with Colin Farrell and are now both fascinated with selkies. It was the most perfect day. I've never, ever been blissfully happy like this before. At one point, on our bike ride, James was a little ways in front of me and as I watched him peddling along the farm roads of Scotland, I thought back to the life I had just left; I thought how this moment would never have happened had I stayed. I have no regrets about leaving. I know it was the right choice, and not once since I left have I cried myself to sleep for missing that life. But this life ends tomorrow. I fly out to London, and then on to Oregon on July 19. It's time to go home and deal with the legal side of divorce. I don't want to leave this life; my heart trembles at the thought of it.

July 15, 2011

Fuck. I'm back to this shitty feeling. My heart is breaking. Fucking again. Sometimes I hate that I feel everything so damn deeply. I'm sitting in this tiny airplane, trying so desperately not to cry, and my heart is absolutely breaking. I feel hollow. My heart stopped beating the moment I walked away from the ship, away from James. Never before have I felt this...emptiness...when saying goodbye to a man. I'm spending four days in London before going 'home', wherever home may be. For now, it's Oregon, and I'm sick at the thought of being there. That place is not my home; it never has been. I need these four days in London. It feels like I left the ship ages ago when in reality, it was only twelve hours. My life on the ship, and James, feel like a distant memory already; like another lifetime. As does my life in Japan. My life has changed so drastically, in so many ways, in the past 12 months. I'm exhausted. What will happen when I get back to Oregon? I'm in a position to completely reinvent my life; I can go anywhere, do anything. I'll do anything to not have to stay in Oregon for too long. But what will I do? Go back to Bellingham? Back to Grizzly Industrial? Get an apartment? Get stuck with nearly the same life I walked out on? Deciding on a path has always been the hardest part for me. I never know which direction to go.

July 18, 2011

I'm sitting on public stairs somewhere in London, near Westminster. I'm so thankful I decided to take these days in London. I need to be alone, away from everything familiar, and grieve; grieve for leaving the ship, for leaving my friends. I can't believe I'll be in Oregon in less than 24 hours. I feel so fragile right now. I've walked this city for the past eleven hours straight, in the rain, listening to my music, my tears hidden by raindrops. I'm sick of writing, but I always seem to come back to it, especially when I'm traveling alone, which I always find myself doing. I simply cannot find the words to express how I feel right now. I'm scared to go home. I'm incredibly grateful for my parents; I don't know what I would do without them, but Oregon suffocates me with terrible memories. Driving past my brother's grave always chokes me.

July 20, 2011

I'm on a plane from San Francisco to Medford, Oregon. My cousin, Whendi, was meant to collect me from the airport but she has to work, so my mom is picking me up. Am I going to be able to hold it together in front of her? I feel like it would be okay to break down in front of Whendi, but not in front of my mom. Why is that? She's such a strong woman, and she's been through some bullshit so she gets it. She's the one who taught me how to be strong, to be independent. I suppose I don't want her to see how broken I am right now. I feel like ancient china, so fragile and threatening to slip through delicate fingers at any moment and shatter upon the floor. After Japan, I started taking anti-depressants, but I stopped taking them on the ship due to my overdose on pure joy. And I knew I would need them when I left the ship. I started taking them again today. I'm a wreck. All I can think about is dancing with James in the crew mess, walking the streets of ancient Mediterranean cities with my friends, existing upon the waves and seeing dolphins in the wild nearly every day. Where will I go from here? What will I do? How will I live? I have no money, no job, no home. This feeling of uncertainty is terrifying, but it's better than the feeling of drowning in the American Dream like I was.

July 30, 2011

I no longer count stairs. And I've started reading books again. All my years I've had this bizarre quirk of counting stairs in my head when I go up or down, even the same staircases I walk every day and know by memory how many stairs there are. I've never been able to stop myself from doing it. On the ship, I stopped, and I haven't started again. Why is that? Was it because I was walking stairs between the decks continuously on the Steve? Was it because I was so busy that my mind didn't have time to count? I haven't been able to read a book since returning from Japan. I found that I simply couldn't concentrate. My eyes would be reading the words, my hands turning the pages, but my mind would be in Japan and I'd have to back up and re-read several pages when I caught myself drifting. I've always been a reader, and I missed my connection with books. But I'm finally reading again, and feeling a book in my hands is so soothing. I need to feel soothed right now. I feel like I'll crumble at any moment...

August 17, 2011

Ah, the illusion has been shattered. My heart is broken. I had a disagreement with Scott from Sea Shepherd and he "removed" me from the organization. But it's not just that – he brought everyone into it; all my fellow Cove Guardians from Japan, all my crewmates from the Steve Irwin. He emailed them all and told them not to have any further contact with me. I'm so tired, and I feel so goddamned alone. I gave everything to that organization; I gave up everything and at the first sign of my questioning them, they turned on me. Scott turned on me and is trying to destroy me, to destroy my reputation. This is what people were warning me about, and I knew that Sea Shepherd does this to people; makes them feel loved and included until they willingly sign their lives over (there actually is a waiver that each crew member signs stating that if they die, SSCS is not liable), then they take advantage of their passion, their loyalty, their lost-ness, and eventually throw them out on their asses when they're no longer useful - broken and alone and financially destitute from years of being a volunteer. I've seen it happen time and again, good people, questioning the morality of what we're asked to do in the name of "conservation", only to be kicked out, shunned. Left devastated. But I never believed it would happen to me. Scott was my friend. Paul was my friend. Now Scott is savagely attacking me, and Paul won't return my emails. All of it, everything I had while aboard the Steve, the friendships I forged, the security I felt...ALL OF IT WAS AN ILLUSION. Sea Shepherd is disgusting. My friend and ex-Sea Shepherd volunteer Pete Bethune was absolutely correct when he called them "morally bankrupt". The things I saw happen on the ship were a disgrace. Paul turned his back on me when I needed him; he buried his head in the sand while Scott tore me apart. The money. The power. The fame. The women. None of it is pure anymore. None of it is about the whales anymore.

I Roam

I have sailed the mighty seas

And walked paths through great countries

The Earth is my home

And alone, I roam

To the furthest corners

The most obscure borders

My memories are currency

Outweighing the value of any coin

I trade possession for experience

Magical moments in cobblestoned alleys

Ancient cities dripping with history

The Earth is my home

And alone, I roam

I've seen more than you can imagine

More than I can remember

I've lived deeply and freely

With the beauty of life saturating my soul

I roam

With the vast Earth my home

Let Go and Fall

But if you just leave, like I'm so good at

You'll find out, these bittersweet memories

They leave tears on your skin

Hard to control when they begin

I can't help myself, when there's an escape

I keep my secrets with the stars

Trying to find an in between

And wanting to fall back in love eventually

I shiver as it all crumbles and breaks

I whisper as it all falls apart

And I let go, finally

I let go, and fall

Don't try to find me

When I run, like I always do

Don't try to follow me, I would let you down

My storms will rage on

And I'll never be safe, in your arms

The Mountain, The Moon, And You

Clouds above the mountains

And skipping stones in the river

Beneath the halo of the moon

I can smell it in the air

And feel it on the wind

Whatever this is, it's not ending

I whisper to the moon

As you hold my hand in your sleep

The violin drifts as my heart sinks

I want the light to come down

From the ring around the moon

While the fire burns bright

You let yourself hide

While I sing to the mountain

Listen to the rhythm of our hearts

Because to me, everything is you

You

Like the river rushing by

Smoothing the stones of their sharp edges

Like the alpenglow

Wrapping the glaciers in fiery pink light

Like the wind between the aspen leaves

Would I notice any of it, if I were still looking at you?

I see the jagged peaks dancing against the dusk

And the waves, reaching their salty fingers toward the shore

Would all of it be lost to me

If you were still all I could see?

Wrapped in a cloak of grey

You were the one I wanted to stay

But as I look at you now, your eyes, your heart

They've gone away

I drift out to sea, remembering our beginning

Thank You

My first thank you absolutely must go to Emily Whittenagen. It is because of her that I finally finished writing this book. Her inspiration, her guidance, friendship, and amazing editing skills are the reason this book became a reality.

And to Jackie, for not only reading all my drafts of this book and giving me her valuable input, but for being a real and true friend. Jackie – I thought you didn't like me when I first started working at the Sea Bean. I've never been happier to have been so wrong.

For my dear friends Robert Wynia, David Amador, and Peter Cornett ~ I would not exist as the person I am today if it weren't for the three of you following your dreams of making music. No matter how far I am from the Pacific Northwest, I carry you with me always and am eternally soothed by the beautiful tunes of Floater. Rob, words cannot encompass what it means to have your words grace these pages; there is no one in the world more appropriate to write the foreword for this book. It is an honor to be your friend.

To all my friends in the Puget Sound region of Washington State; there are too many to name, but you know who you are. There is no doubt that Whatcom and Island counties are enchanted, and I feel blessed to call that area my home. No matter how far and wide I may roam, my heart will always rest in the PNW, and I will forever remember the encouragement and support that I received from each of you.

To my nomad friends the world over ~ you are my family that I have collected along the way, my Souvenir Friends, and though I may never see many of you again, you are in my heart forever. Thank you for the nurturing environment of understanding and a shared passion for truly living. I am a better person for having each of you in my life, no matter how brief it may have been.

To everyone I grew up with in the Rogue Valley of Southern Oregon ~ thank you for the childhood we shared. No one can ever take those memories away from us.

And where would I be without you, Admiral? You are the absolute best thing to come out of The Boat Company for me. Your friendship, your guidance, and your patience light up my life. Thank you for tutoring me while I was in Sea School, and for imparting your maritime wisdom upon me (sorry I hit the dock in the zodiac that one time. Oops).

And of course, for my Mom and Dad. My number one fans, my biggest supporters, my unfailing entourage. Thank you isn't enough; there are no words that would ever be enough. I am who I am because of the two of you. I love you both more than I could ever express.

The homeless kids of Seward, Alaska – Matty, Corbin, Liberty, and Ashley

Liberty and Bryan sit on the floor of the Sea Bean Café staff house

Part of the Sea Bean Café staff

Kayaking Resurrection Bay in Seward. Photo by Liberty

Bonfires on the beach in Seward. Photo by Liberty

209

Liberty and Jackie in Anchorage, Alaska

Liberty and her Jeep. Photo by Sam Vaughan

Liberty stands at the Cove in Japan on Christmas day, 2010

The Cove. Taiji, Japan. Photo by Liberty

Dead dolphins are hauled from the gutting barge at the Cove. Photo by Liberty

Liberty and a fellow Cove Guardian are questioned by Japanese police at the Cove

Liberty is photographed by a Japanese reporter as she looks out over
the dolphin sea pens in the Taiji harbor

A Cove Guardian swims in the Cove as dolphins are being driven in.
Photo by Liberty

Liberty and her assistant, Nicole, at the Cove

Liberty at a circus protest she organized during her time living in
Australia

Liberty and conservationist Ric O'Barry, star of the documentary,
The Cove. Miami, Florida

Liberty with ex-SeaWorld trainer, John Hargrove, star of the
documentary, Blackfish, at the release of the beer Liberty created,
Lolita Orca Ale, brewed by Kulshan Brewing in Bellingham,
Washington. The beer was made as a way to raise awareness for
Lolita, an orca in captivity. Proceeds benefitted the Orca Network.

Liberty with the band, Floater, in Seattle

Liberty with Pete and Rob from Floater. Medford, OR

Liberty and Teresa in the place where Bern was killed. Wimer, Oregon

Liberty and her editor/friend, Emily, in the engine room of the Liseron

Liberty aboard the Liseron in Southeast Alaska. 2014

Swimming in the ocean, Southeast Alaska and Hawaii

"This world has gone, and drug us along, and nothing's the same, and it will never be again. It's never gonna be the same" Floater

Born and raised in the Pacific Northwest, Liberty Miller grew up with a deep love of nature, the ocean in particular.

She lives in her converted Dodge van and roams to wherever life wants to take her. She has lived in several different countries, and all over the United States.

Currently, the majority of her time is divided between Seattle, Washington and Seward, Alaska.

Visit her website at www.libertyeliasmiller.com or email her at theheartoftherunaway@gmail.com

For more information about The Boat Company, visit their website at www.theboatcompany.org

Made in the USA
Monee, IL
29 December 2019